- Where are you now?
- I'm taking a nice hike on a beautiful mountain trail. What are you doing?
- I'm here at the beach, relaxing and having a good time.
- I wish I was there with you, but I can't stand the hot sun.
- That's all right. I don't want to spend all day tramping through the woods. Have fun.
- Next year we should plan a vacation we'd both enjoy together.
- Great! How about shopping?
- Hmm... How about bear hunting?

I wish these women would stop making so much noise so I could do my job in peace.

This glass ceiling is hard to crack, but if we keep hammering away it will come down in pieces.

Maybe we should forget about hammers and start using dynamite.

Whew! This is hard work. Maybe I should have stayed home.
It took me four hours to get to the top. I guess now I found a shortcut. I'll be down in no time!

Help!
I'm drowning!
Save me.
I don't want to get wet.
I have an important
lunch date.
Hold on! I'm coming! I'll teach
myself to swim on the way.

The Best Reading & Discussion Textbook for

Intermediate and Advanced English Users!!!

3rd Edition
All New

EXPRESS YOURSELF 1

15 Practical Topics 15 Dialogs

958 Questions to Make You Think
31 Opinion Samples
Plus 180 Captions
Everything You Need to Learn Real English!
Express Yourself & Improve Yourself

Written by LIS KOREA Editorial Staff &
Duane Vorhees

LIS KOREA

Introduction

NEW: Something that is fresh.

EXPRESS: Fast, direct.

YOURSELF: The most important part of the title, actually. Like the "old" EXPRESS YOURSELF, the new one inspires you to be YOURSELF. Unlike the pre-programmed, robotic texts in common use, NEW EXPRESS YOURSELF encourages you to use English to express your own ideas, emotions, and personality. It insists that you be YOURSELF, not just an anonymous cog in a wheel or a rat in a maze. Other books can provide you with English grammar, but NEW EXPRESS YOURSELF lets you actually use the language you've learned. If you are too self-consciously concerned about making minor syntactical or verbal mistakes, you will not be free to speak your mind freely. So, for real discussion of important issues in your own life and in the world around you, try NEW EXPRESS YOURSELF!

Duane Vorhees

Contents

ISSUE 01

Lifestyles

People have different attitudes toward living. Some seek self-centered* happiness, without any consideration for others. To them, "happiness" means wielding* political or economic power over others. But most of these people turn out to be disappointed in their pursuit of happiness: Since man's desire is endless, nothing can fully satisfy their needs.

Other people believe that the first step to attaining happiness is to restrict personal desire. Priests, monks, and nuns are the most common representatives* of this group. By refraining* from worldly* passion, they think they are happy because they live their lives in accordance with* religious commands. But, can anyone without personal autonomy* be genuinely happy?

A third group consists of very ordinary people. They have no great wealth or political authority. While they may have religious beliefs, they do not turn their backs* on the world. They treasure their families, and they value the little things of everyday life. They are happy if they have three meals a day, a car (even a used car), a home, a vacation, enough money to educate their children....

Which group of people is the happiest? Who knows? If you think you are happy, then you are. Happiness is the result of how you think of yourself and the world you live in.

self-centered : interested only in yourself and not really caring what is happening to other people
wield : have and use (power, influence, etc.) **representative :** (sb/sth) that is typical of a group
refrain : not do (sth) you want to do **worldly :** relating to the human world and ordinary life rather than to religious or spiritual matters **in accordance with :** in a way that agrees with or follows
autonomy : ability to make your own decisions without being influenced by anyone else
turn your back on (sth) : refuse to be involved with (sth)

Comprehension

1. What is a "worldly passion"?
2. Who is the happiest person?
3. Are religious people the only ones who are truly happy?

Express  Yourself

1. When is the best time of the day for you?
2. What do you do when you have some free time? Do you prefer spending it alone or with friends?
3. What types of social activities do you engage in?
4. What do you usually do on weekends?
5. Do you like to travel? Where have you been?
6. Which do you enjoy the most, coffee or tea? Something else?
7. Do you like music? Do you enjoy singing? What musical instruments can you play?
8. Have you ever volunteered to help others? What did you do? How did you feel?
9. Are you usually on time for dates? What do you think about the people who are usually late for appointments?
10. Are you a moviegoer, or do you prefer watching movies at home? What kinds of films do you like?
11. These days cooking programs on TV are very popular. Do you think cooking is an important skill that both men and women should have?
12. Some people say we don't have to cook at home because all kinds of ready-made foods are on the market. Do you agree?
13. Do you think you are frugal*? Why or why not?
14. Do you think the quality of your life is improving or getting worse? Why?
15. Do you think you are happy? Why or why not?
16. What is your life philosophy?
17. What would you think about becoming a priest, monk, or nun?
18. People like to have relationships with other people as much as possible. However, some say the more relationships you have, the more disappointed you are by them. Do you agree? Why or why not?
19. Do you think your future will be better than your present? Why or why not?

---

frugal : using money or supplies in a very careful way

Opinion Samples

1. The quality of my life is worsening, even as I have more money to spend. Of course, material wealth grows as the economy expands. But I don't think money is everything in terms of* the quality of life, which depends upon environmental factors, stress levels, crime rates, education, job satisfaction, and personal relationships. We all know our environment is becoming dirtier and crime is on the rise*. And everybody suffers from* stress, caused by a variety of sources, which shortens life expectancy* and increases illness — even material comfort can be a source of stress! So, the quality of life can't be measured* by material wealth.

2. I can't imagine my life being any better than it is right now! My parents give me a lot of freedom but are still a very protective force for me. I don't have much money to spend, but usually if I want something I just have to ask for it. My grades are okay, and I don't have to study excessively to achieve them, so I have a great deal of free time to devote to* my friends and interests. I have some excellent friends — and I have a Significant Other* who loves me! What more could I ever ask for?

in terms of (sth) : as far as (sth) is concerned
on the rise : increasing in amount, number, level, etc.
suffer from : experience pain, illness, or injury
life expectancy : average number of years that a person or animal can expect to live
measure : judge the importance, value, or extent of (sth)
devote to (sb) : use (time, money, energy, attention, etc.) for (sb)
significant other : (sb) that you have a romantic relationship with

Dialog

Spending Lives Together Apart

Martha : Why don't you come to bed with me?

Tom : I'm not tired. Why don't you stay up* and watch the rest of this movie with me?

Martha : I'd like to, but I can't keep my eyes open a moment longer.

Tom : Well, okay. I'll tell you how it turns out*.

Martha : Please don't. I'll just watch it later, by myself.

Tom : We hardly ever spend any time together anymore.

Martha : Some of my friends' husbands are never home; they're always away on business. You never go anywhere, but I don't see very much of you.

Tom : It's our schedules. You get up early —

Martha : I have to fix* breakfast for you and the kids.

Tom : And I stay up late to read and watch TV.

Martha : Sometimes you don't go to bed until it's time for me to get up!

Tom : Your friends seem to spend their married lives in different time zones, but in a sense so do we!

Martha : Yes, that's right.

QUESTIONS

1. Are you an early bird* or a night owl*?
2. How much sleep is enough for you? Do you ever suffer from insomnia*?
3. How much control do you have over your sleep schedule?

---

stay up : continue to be awake past the time you usually go to bed
turn out : happen, end, or develop in a particular way
fix : make (sth) such as a meal ready
early bird : (sb) who rises, arrives, or acts before the usual or expected time
night owl : (sb) who enjoys staying up late at night
insomnia : inability to sleep

Read & Discuss

Carpe Diem* [Seize the Day] or Not

A close friend exemplifies* the "Live for Today" motto. He is one of the most interesting people I know. Despite his youth, he has traveled widely. He has lots of nice clothes and wonderful possessions, and is always generous when we go out together. To him, money is like water; as long as he has any, he gets whatever he wants and does whatever he wishes. But whenever he is unemployed, he has to borrow from me and other friends to eat and pay his rent. So far, he has managed to keep busy most of the time, but I worry about what will happen to him as he gets older or becomes sick; he obviously* has not acquired any savings.

Another close friend is "Ms Rainy Day." She is always busy working, so it's very hard to spend much time together. She is not miserly* or cheap*, but she has a very careful budget that she sticks to. As a result, she doesn't have many new clothes, and she deprives herself of* a lot of nice things she would like to have. But she insists that she has to prepare for the future, just in case something unexpected happens; she wants to be ready financially for anything.

I'm reminded of the story about the ant and the grasshopper. The grasshopper spent all summer having a good time, while the ant slaved away* continuously. But when winter came, the ant was ready for the cold weather, and the grasshopper starved to death. However, one of the other ants also worked for most of the summer, with no time for enjoyment or relaxation — he had a heart attack* and died before he ever had a chance to take advantage of all the food that he had saved up for the winter.

QUESTIONS

1. Do you regret not doing something when you had the chance?
2. Did some impulsive* act on your part ever deprive you of some future or present comfort?
3. Which motto* best describes your own attitude?

---

carpe diem (Latin) : seize the day; enjoy the present exemplify : show (sth) very clearly
obvious : easy to see or notice miserly : hating to spend money cheap : not willing to share or spend money deprive (sb) of (sth) : take (sth) away from (sb) slave away : work very hard
heart attack : serious medical condition in which (sb's) heart suddenly stops working

The Ups and Downs of Life

Man: Everybody's life has its ups* and downs*, right?

Friend: Sure.

Man: But it seems like some people mainly have ups and more ups, while others have downs and more downs.

Friend: Well, some people are good at turning their downs into ups while others make even ups downs.

QUESTIONS

1. What are some examples of how people reverse* their ups and downs?
2. What are the main causes* of your own ups and downs?
3. Do you know how to make downs ups, or do you routinely* make your ups downs?

---

impulsive : doing things suddenly and without careful thought; forceful
motto : short statement that expresses the aims or beliefs of (sb)
ups: state of success, happiness, etc. downs : state of failure, trouble, etc.
reverse : change (sth) to an opposite state or condition
cause : (sth) that produces an effect, result, or condition routinely : usually

Points to Ponder

1

The world is full of people making a good living but making poor lives.

2

In the story of life, death is not a period but a comma.

3

It has been said that life is a game — but how can we play it if we don't know where the goalposts are?

4

Some people treat life like a slot machine* — putting in as little as possible while hoping for a lucky jackpot*.

---

slot machine : machine used for gambling that starts when you put coins into it and pull a handle or press a button

jackpot : usually large amount of money won in a game of chance

The following sentences are all related thematically. They express a wide difference of opinions and attitudes. You may agree with some of them and disagree with others. Please discuss what you think the sentences mean and what you think about them.

5

The tragedy* of life is what dies inside a man while he lives.

6

Rich or poor, we must be aware that we will not be ready to meet* the blows* which will surely come.

7

Design your life yourself or be content* with being part of someone else's plan. (And guess what they have planned for you? Not much.)

8

A tiger doesn't lose sleep over the opinion of sheep.

tragedy : very bad event that causes great sadness
meet : deal with or face (sth) directly
blow : sudden shock or disappointment
content : happy and satisfied

1

Don't I look wonderful?
Why don't you buy me and
show me off to your friends?

I think if I just
work another hour
or two a day, I could
get another 10%
raise in my salary.
My kids would
hardly miss me.

Life is too hard.
I didn't know how
I could face every
day if I were sober*.

sober : not drunk

2

Everyone dies someday. We all live our
lives in a coffin*. But the question is,
is that the end? Or is there some sort
of life after death?

coffin : box in which a dead person is buried

3
I don't know.
Where's the ball?
Did the other team
already go home?
Where's
the goalpost?
I wonder how many
people know how to
play the game properly.

4
Hey, kid, don't bother
with putting money in
that piggy bank.
It takes too
long for
pennies to
become
a fortune.
Maybe so. But it
won't take you long
to lose everything.

5

I just got a great promotion* that I would not have got if I had spent more time with my family. How fortunate I am!

promotion : move to a more important job or rank in a company or organization

6

Nobody told me there would be rocks in my path. I thought that life would be a smooth ride and gravity* would do all the work.

gravity : force that causes things to fall toward the Earth

on (sb's) account : because of (sb)
snore : breathe noisily while sleeping

ISSUE 02

Good Habits & Bad

Rather than sudden, grave resolution*, your life is probably more affected by trivial*, repetitive, unthinking* behavior. Until the day you die, your body and mind will be governed* by good habits and bad ones. These acts determine* the quality of your existence. Everyone knows that bad habits are easy to form, since they are quite agreeable* to man's lazy and selfish nature; but good ones are difficult to fabricate* because they need perseverance* and lack social reinforcement*. Nevertheless, though bad habits are hard to break, it is never too late to start making good ones — you just need determination and dedication*. Doing something over and over again until you don't have to think about it is how actions become habitual in the first place.

---

resolution : promise to yourself that you will make a serious effort to do (sth) that you should do
trivial : not important
unthinking : done or said in a foolish or careless way without thinking about the possible effects
govern : control or guide   determine : influence or decide
agreeable : pleasing to the mind or senses   fabricate : make or produce
perseverance : steadfastness in doing (sth) despite difficulty or delay in achieving success
reinforcement : process of encouraging or establishing a belief or pattern of behavior
dedication : hard work or effort that (sb) puts into a particular activity

Comprehension

1. Is "habit" ever directly defined in the paragraph?
2. Why are bad habits so easy to acquire?
3. What would make it easier to form good habits?

Express  Yourself

1. What are your good and bad habits?
2. What are the good habits you wanted to get but failed and the bad habits you tried to crack* in vain*?
3. What are the good habits we all should develop, from the time we are little kids?
4. How do we create a habit? Or does it just happen without any activity on our part?
5. What good habits do you want your children to develop? What bad habits do they already have?
6. What good habits do you want your boyfriend or girlfriend to have? What are the bad habits they have?
7. What habits lead you to success? What habits to failure?
8. Some say "little" habits determine whether or not you succeed. Explain what this means.

More Talking Points (1)

In the following activities, what habits would be good (and bad) in their exercise*?

a. driving
b. reading
c. watching TV
d. studying English
e. talking with people
f. spending money
g. shopping
h. exercising
i. sleeping
j. drinking
k. eating
l. using a smart phone

crack : stop doing (sth) that you have regularly done for a long time, esp. (sth) that is bad for you
in vain : without success in spite of your efforts
exercise : activity or process

Opinion Samples

1. Though I'm not even aware of most of my habits — they just happen naturally — sometimes I have taught myself to do things automatically. Like getting up early in the morning. I have done this for so long that I no longer need an alarm clock. Unfortunately, I get up even on holidays when I could sleep in*. But all habit acquisition* comes from training. Force yourself to do the same thing at the same time under the same circumstances every day, and it doesn't take very long to make it a habit.

2. People watch too much television — or, rather, they don't watch it at all in any meaningful sense. They turn it on indiscriminately* and then leave it on whether or not they are watching it. It's on, making noise, whether they are eating or talking to each other or taking a nap*. So people should carefully limit their TV time to a few shows they really want — sports or news or whatever — and spend the rest of their time more actively engaged: reading a book, playing a musical instrument, or taking a walk.

3. Merchandisers know that most purchases are spot* decisions rather than carefully considered acts. We all buy things we don't really need and spend too much for them. So we should devise* a careful budget every week or every month and stick to* it, avoiding temptation* by leaving our cash and credit cards at home when we go out. If we absolutely have to get something, we should plan our moves as carefully as a general* preparing an attack: What do we need exactly, how much are we willing to spend, and where can we get it the cheapest?

sleep in : deliberately sleep later than usual in the morning
acquisition : learning or developing of a skill, habit, or quality
indiscriminate : not careful in making choices
nap : short period of sleep, esp. during the day
spot : immediate
devise : plan
stick to : not change (a decision, belief, etc.)
temptation : strong urge or desire to have or do (sth)
general : military officer of very high rank

Dialog

Trading Habits

Doug : You used to have my dinner ready for me when I got home, but you don't anymore. What happened?

Connie : I never knew what time you were coming home, so I just got out of* the habit.

Doug : If I promise to be here at the same time every day, can you promise to cook for me again?

Connie : Of course! I love cooking for you! But I thought you never really cared. I'm not your slave, after all.

Doug : No, I love your cooking! I'm sorry that I never let you know how much I appreciate your hard work.

Connie : Nobody likes to be taken for granted*.

Doug : You know, sometimes I feel the same way. I come home after a long day and you just ignore me.

Connie : We just got too used to each other, so we stopped trying to improve our relationship.

Doug : You're right. We need to develop some new habits, I guess.

Connie : And get rid of* some old, bad habits too.

Doug : Such as?

Connie : You should stop smoking. It's bad for your health, and it makes everything stink*.

Doug : I've been smoking for 20 years! It will be hard to quit. But if it will make you happy, I'll try.

Connie : Thank you. But it's also for your sake*.

Doug : I'm sure you're right. But you should cut back on your overeating, for the same reasons. It's not good for your health, and it destroys your good looks.

Connie : I eat when I'm bored and depressed. It's lonely here all day with no one to talk to, and when you get home, you don't talk. You just turn on the TV and go to sleep.

Doug : I guess we both need to develop some new habits.

Connie : I'll try if you will.

Doug : It's a deal*! Maybe we can each reinforce* the other's efforts and this won't be so hard.

It takes persistent effort to keep a lawn trim* and tidy*. Or we wouldn't be able to get the fruit due to the weeds.

If I give enough attention to this plant, it will flower and bloom. Someday we can eat the fruit.

QUESTIONS

1. Do you think we deliberately* form bad habits, or do they just happen?
2. What do you think is the most important change that Doug or Connie needs to make?
3. What will be the easiest change for either one of them to accomplish?

---

get out of (sth) : stop having (a habit) **take (sb/sth) for granted :** fail to properly notice or appreciate
get rid of : throw away; remove **stink :** have a very bad smell **for your sake :** out of consideration for you
it's a deal : agreed **reinforce :** encourage or give support to (sth) **trim :** neat and orderly
tidy : clean and organized **deliberate :** intended or planned

Read & Discuss

Essential Habits to Be a Successful Person

"Success" means the acquisition of wealth to most people, but in fact it does not have to be thought of in those terms. Success can be the achievement of a skill, a personal goal, or a state of mind. But no matter how it is defined, it can be promoted* by developing a few good habits.

1. Decide what you want to be or get, and stay focused on that. Don't let yourself get distracted*.
2. Before you retire* for the night, make note of everything you did that day to further* your goal, and everything you did to interfere with* it.
3. Begin each new day by trying to project* the actions you can take to promote your ambition.
4. Be flexible* and realistic*. Reevaluate your desire and your progress on the first day of every month.
5. Keep records of your progress that you can review and reevaluate on a regular basis.
6. It's okay to pursue more than one goal at a time. But be sure not to try too many at once.
7. Be patient and persistent. Don't expect instant gratification*.

If you make this process habitual and automatic, you will definitely succeed most of the time!

I have many steps ahead of me, more than I know. But there are many more behind. Going back again is harder than going forward.

QUESTIONS

1. Do you think this deliberate means of developing habits can work? Why or why not?
2. Would you be willing to wholeheartedly* subject* yourself to it?
3. Are there any other habits that should be added to the process?

promote : help (sth) happen, develop, or increase distracted : unable to concentrate
retire : go to bed further : help the progress of (sth) interfere with (sth) : stop or slow (sth)
project : plan flexible : willing to change or to try different things
realistic : based on what is real rather than on what is wanted or hoped for; sensible and appropriate
gratification : satisfaction wholehearted : showing complete sincerity and commitment
subject (sb) : force (sb) to experience (sth) harmful, unpleasant, etc.

When Habits Become Obsessions*

Man: I usually wash my hands more than 100 times a day. I hate the idea of having germs. I think that is a good habit, but many others call it an obsessive-compulsive disorder*. What should I do?

Friend: There is no clear-cut* distinction*. If you think it's just a habit, you don't need to see a doctor, but if you think it's an obsession you should.

— It's easy to walk on the rope when you maintain good balance.
— But falling off is even easier!
— Maybe so. But I'll get safely to the other side, and you'll just get wet, or maybe drown.

QUESTIONS

1. What's the difference between a habit and an obsession?
2. Do you have anything you're obsessed about?
3. Talk about some "good obsessions."

---

obsession : state in which (sb) thinks about (sb/sth) constantly or frequently, esp. in a way that is not normal
obsessive-compulsive disorder : mental illness that involves repeating actions or thinking about certain things too much
clear-cut : very obvious and sharp
distinction : clear difference between things

Points to Ponder

1

The worst boss anyone can have is a bad habit.

2

Good habits are usually formed; bad habits we fall into*.

3

Many people look forward to* the new year for a new start on old habits.

4

Ninety-nine percent of failure comes from people who have the habit of making excuses.

---

fall into : begin to do without trying to do
look forward to (sth) : expect (sth) with pleasure

The following sentences are all related thematically. They express a wide difference of opinions and attitudes. You may agree with some of them and disagree with others. Please discuss what you think the sentences mean and what you think about them.

5

Laziness is nothing more than the habit of resting before you get tired.

6

Stop the habit of wishful thinking* and start the habit of thoughtful wishes.

7

As long as habit and routine dictate* the pattern of living, no new dimensions* of the soul will emerge.

8

Only habit can subdue* habit.

---

wishful thinking : attitude or belief that (sth) you want to happen will happen even though it is not likely or possible **dictate :** control or influence **dimension :** aspect or feature
subdue : overcome or bring under control

1

Here's to success! Have a cigar!
Of course! But too much success like this will kill me.

2

Life is good when somebody else has to do all the work.
Just wait! Soon it will be my turn to get the good life. I hope you'll enjoy the effort you'll put into it when we switch places.

3

There's no competition when we run each new race on the good habits we've created.

4

[Loser's Olympics]

5

I eat before I'm hungry and drink before I'm thirsty. Now I hope somebody wakes me up when it's time to go to bed so I can sleep.

6

Why don't you go to work? What happened to all your dreams?

I still have the dreams, whenever I'm asleep. Having them when I'm awake is the hard part.

7

I run, run, run, but I never get anywhere.

I keep climbing because I know I can get to the top.

8

I don't understand. I've always won because I'm bigger than everyone else.

But you got so big by eating too much. You should have trained harder and kept fit. But now it's too late.

ISSUE 03
Health

People say that health is the most important thing in life, but it seems to have the least significance in their actual lives. Indeed, most people actually undermine* their health through lack of exercise and unbalanced diets. Alcohol, smoking, and junk food also aggravate* this phenomenon.

Another factor that adds to people's health problems is stress. Experts say we can't avoid stress as long as we live in this ever-changing world. So what counts* is not how to avoid it, but how to reduce it and cope with it effectively. Environmental issues* — low air or water quality — also negatively impact* us.

On the other hand, modern medical researchers still suspect our genes* have considerable* control over our destiny. We all have a genetic tendency toward certain conditions. This means our health is still in the hands of God. However, that doesn't necessarily mean we can't do anything about our bodies. Rather, we should continue to stay fit by temperate* living — no smoking, moderate drinking, a nutritional diet, and adequate exercise. That way, to some extent, we can compensate* for our genetically undesirable aspects.

---

undermine : make (sb/sth) less strong or effective aggravate : make (sth) more serious or severe
count : have value or importance
issues : problems or concerns
impact : have an important or noticeable effect on (sb/sth)
gene : basic physical unit of heredity
considerable : large in size, amount, or quantity
temperate : showing moderation or self-restraint
compensate : provide (sth) good as a balance against (sth) bad or undesirable

Comprehension

1. Is personal behavior more (or less) important than genetic factors in terms of* health?
2. Does the environment play any role? How?
3. If someone says, "My health is in the hands of God," what does he mean?

Express  Yourself

1. Do you think you are healthy?
2. Do you eat three balanced meals a day?
3. Do you take vitamins every day? Do you think they improve your health?
4. Do you often drink a tonic*? If so, what is it? Why do you drink it?
5. Do you exercise every day? Why or why not?
6. If you work out too much, you are likely to get addicted to exercise. Can you define what exercise addiction is? Is it dangerous?
7. What are your everyday stresses? Do you cope with them well?
8. Have you ever been hospitalized? If so, why? For how long?
9. Do you regularly see a dentist? Why or why not?
10. When you have a cold, do you see a doctor right away, just rest at home, or try to ignore it?
11. Do you trust doctors?
12. What disease are you the most afraid of?
13. What do you think is the most important thing in terms of your own health?
14. Lack of exercise and poor diet are the main culprits* leading to bad health. Do you think you are well-balanced with both aspects?
15. Do you think fasting* is good for your health?
16. Do you believe in faith healing*? Why or why not?
17. Do you think cancer will be conquered* in the near future?
18. How much do you think your genes affect your health?
19. How can we define mental health?
20. How are physical and mental health related? Do they affect each other?

---

in terms of : with regard to the particular aspect or subject specified tonic : medical substance taken to give a feeling of vigor or well-being culprit : cause of a problem or defect fast : eat no food for a period of time faith healing : healing achieved by religious belief and prayer, rather than by medical treatment conquer : gain control of (sth) through great effort

Opinion Samples

1. Doctors are useful tools and should be employed accordingly*. They are available* to prescribe* medicines we cannot purchase on our own, and they are handy* for performing serious procedures, like surgery, that we lack the skill and practice to perform. But most of the advice they give us is just common sense: "Get more sleep," "Cut back on your smoking," "Exercise more." It doesn't take an MD* to know those things! I also believe that too many doctors make recommendations that are designed to improve their own economic situation more than their patients' health, by mandating* unnecessary (and expensive) courses of action.

2. A lot of our illnesses are psychological more than physical in nature and thus can be affected by a change in our mental state. We get "well" because we think we are better. But we run the risk of ignoring genuine diseases because we have become convinced that some quack* claiming a supernatural, magical power has done something to cure us. These frauds* prey on* desperate* individuals, and their loved ones, who suffer from a severe malady* that is difficult or impossible to treat successfully. These pitiable* people are willing to try anything, because nothing else works. But they are only enriching a con man* while doing nothing to improve their own condition.

accordingly : in a proper or appropriate way
available : qualified and willing to be of service or assistance
prescribe : advise and authorize the use of (a medicine or treatment) for (sb), esp. in writing
handy : good at using (sth), esp. a tool
MD : Doctor of Medicine
mandate : officially demand or require (sth)
quack : (sb) who dishonestly claims to have special knowledge and skill in some field, typically in medicine
fraud : (sb) intended to deceive others, typically by unjustifiable claiming
prey on (sb) : try to influence, deceive, or harm weaker people
desperate : willing to do anything to change a very bad situation, and not caring about danger
malady : illness
pitiable : deserving pity or sympathy
con man : (sb) who tricks other people in order to get their money

Dialog

Daily Exercise: How Much Is Too Much?

Harold : Why don't you come with me to the gym today?

Maud : I don't have the proper clothing.

Harold : Then we should take a long hike this weekend!

Maud : Sorry. I don't have appropriate footwear.

Harold : How about yoga?

Maud : I don't have the time. I'm too busy at the office this time of year.

Harold : That's exactly the point. You sit around all day and gain weight, and your health suffers as a result. If you led a more active daily life, you would feel a lot better.

Maud : I feel fine. I never miss a day of work, and I do whatever I like afterwards. Except for an occasional cold, I don't have any health problems at all. So I think deliberate* exercise is a waste of time.

Harold : I work out* every day. I take a vigorous* walk every morning before breakfast, and I spend two hours a day at the gym — except on weekends, when I go to the pool instead. And every Sunday I go bowling with my team. On the job, I'm always performing isometric* exercises between work tasks. When I don't have anything else to do, I fill the time with some kind of physical activity.

Maud : When I see you, you usually have some muscle pain or soreness you complain about. You exercise too much, and your body can't keep up anymore. You should slow down and relax more.

Harold : We sure are different in terms of the way we stay healthy. I can't imagine staying fit by avoiding exercise, and you can't see the value of getting any at all.

QUESTIONS

1. How about you? Are you "Maud" or "Harold"? Or neither?
2. Calculate how many hours of physical activity you spend every week. Do you think that is enough?
3. What are your favorite excuses for avoiding physical exercise?

---

deliberate : intended or planned work out : exercise vigorous : done with great force and energy
isometric : relating to muscular action

Read & Discuss

Living and Dying

Health is the one commodity that we cannot buy or trade. We can try to take care of ourselves or we can do our best to destroy ourselves by engaging in unhealthy lifestyles, but in the end it doesn't matter. Sooner or later we are going to acquire a fatal illness. When that happens, we may be old and in poor overall* health, or we may be young and in great shape. But when we know that we are going to die, what are we going to do about it?

One type of person will decide that dying is just part of the natural life cycle and must be endured. Perhaps this attitude is buttressed* by a notion that interfering with the natural or divinely* ordained* course of events is sinful*. They are determined to live as long as possible, even though life itself is painful and without pleasure.

Another type of person will decide that having a right to life also implies a right to end a life of misery. If they know that from now on the condition of their life will continue to deteriorate*, that the pain will increase (or that it can be countered* only by larger and larger doses of opiates*, causing them to lose mental lucidity*), that they will have to lose more and more of their human dignity the longer they hold onto their pathetic* lives, they may decide to take their fate into their own hands. They may prefer to choose to die rather than allow life to become meaningless.

The first type of person may not want to deprive loved ones of his or her presence, while the second type may not want to subject loved ones to the expense and stress of useless care.

But either choice, of stoic* acceptance or of practical euthanasia*, requires a distinct kind of human courage. Neither choice is pleasant.

QUESTIONS

1. Is suicide ever justified?
2. Is life, no matter how poor, always more valuable than anything else?
3. If you were one of the types of persons described above, could you support the decision of a loved one who belonged to the other type?

---

overall : viewed as a whole or in general **buttress :** support, strengthen, or defend (sth)

Let's Talk Funny

Walking to Get Fit

Man: Experts say that 15 minutes of fast walking burns about the same number of calories as 20 minutes of running. It's cheap, convenient, and not likely to cause injury. So why don't people walk more?

Friend: They are too busy to walk.

Man: But they can take the time to drive to the gym and work out there on an expensive treadmill.

Friend: They don't think walking free of charge is a good workout.

QUESTIONS

1. Where do you usually work out?
2. Do you think gym fees are worth the money? Why or why not?
3. What's the difference between doing your exercise at home or in a gym?

---

divine : coming from God **ordain :** officially order **sinful :** wrong according to religious or moral law
deteriorate : become worse as time passes **counter :** make (sth) less effective
opiate : drug that is made from opium and that is used to reduce pain
lucidity : ability to think clearly **pathetic :** causing feelings of sadness and sympathy
stoic : showing no emotion, esp. when (sth) bad is happening
euthanasia : practice of killing (sb) who is very sick or injured in order to prevent any more suffering

Points to Ponder

1

A lot of people lose their health trying to become wealthy, and then lose their riches trying to get their health back.

2

Many people suffer from poor health, not because of what they eat but from what is eating them.

3

The only way to keep your health is to eat what you don't want, drink what you don't like, and do what you'd rather not.

4

The secret of good health is to leave the table hungry, the bed sleepy, and the tavern* thirsty.

---

tavern : place where alcoholic drinks can be bought and drunk

The following sentences are all related thematically. They express a wide difference of opinions and attitudes. You may agree with some of them and disagree with others. Please discuss what you think the sentences mean and what you think about them.

5

He's the best physician that knows the worthlessness of the most medicines.

6

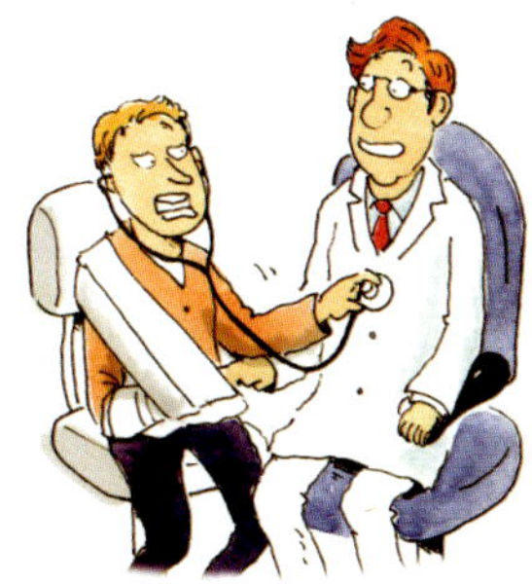

Every patient carries his or her own doctor inside.

7

Overnight stardom can be harmful to your mental health. It has ruined a lot of people.

8

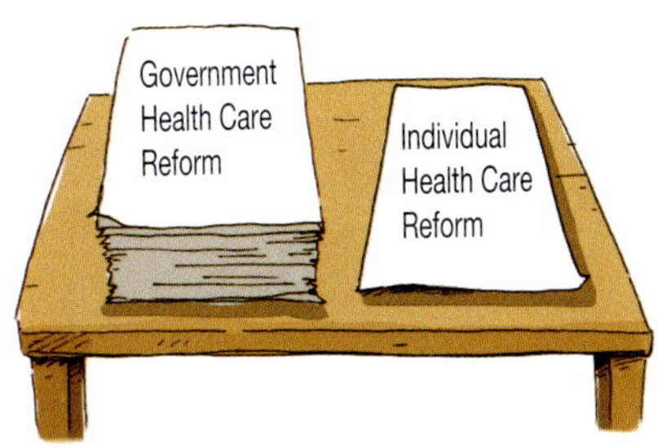

True health care reform cannot happen in government. It has to happen in our kitchens, in our homes, in our communities. All health care is personal.

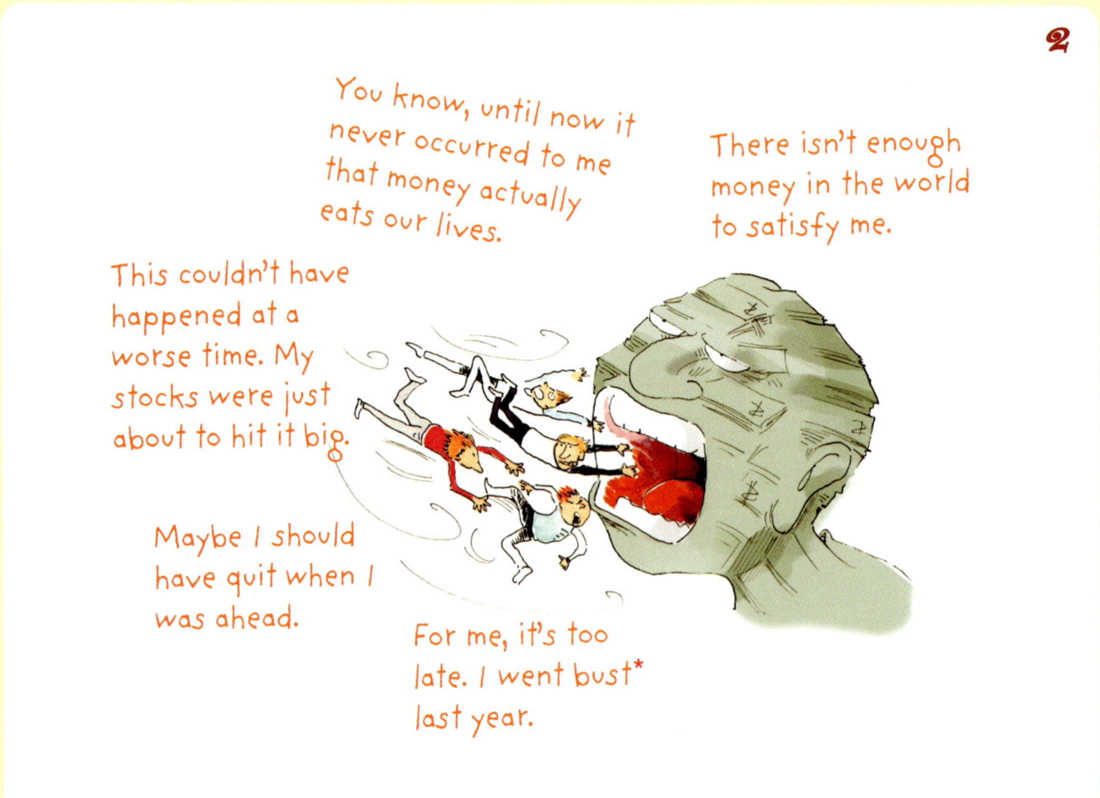

go bust : lose all of your money; go broke

3
Hey, bud, you can have me, all of me.
I'm delicious. A few calories don't matter.
Try me. I'm so refreshing.
Why did my wife and doctor hide my hammer? I can't take this diet anymore.

4
I need to get a new alarm clock. I slept right through my nightly dinner-and-drinks date with my buddies.
Get a new clock! I'm sick and tired of being ignored. Or else, change your bad habits.

5

Mine thought that a good diet would prevent most of my problems.

Mine insisted that a healthy lifestyle was key.

That's right. Now, with this wonderful facility in town, I can hardly wait to get sick.

My old doctor told me that common sense and plenty of exercise would keep me healthy.

I'm tired of my physician always nagging me about my bad habits.

6

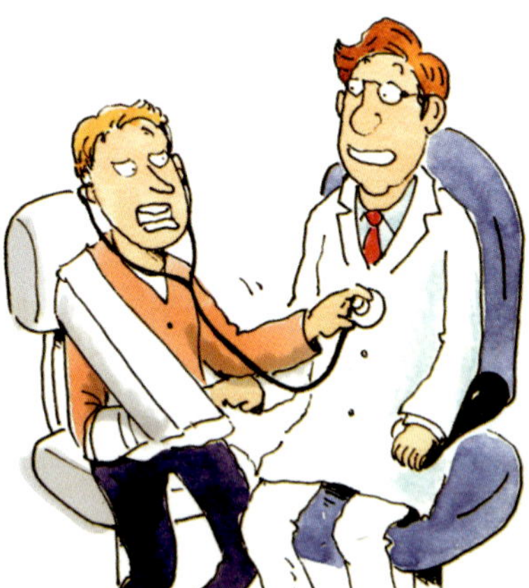

– Nobody knows how I feel better than I do.

– Yes, you know if you're sick or not. But you don't know how to treat yourself.

– I always treat myself to the best.

– Yes, that's your problem. The "best" is not necessarily the best for your health.

7

– I feel very generous today. I just hit the lottery jackpot and I feel guilty about my sudden wealth.

– Don't give me so much. I don't want to get spoiled by unearned riches.

– Yes, instant wealth has ruined a lot of people, but so has lifelong poverty.

– But, rich or poor, I know that I've earned my own destiny.

8

Look at me! I weigh a lot and cost a lot, and I need a lot of bureaucrats* to administer* me.

Big deal*. I hardly weigh anything and cost very little. And I can do most of it by myself.

bureaucrat : official in a government department
administer : manage and be responsible for the running of (a business, organization, etc.)
big deal : impressive (but used here sarcastically, meaning "not impressive")

ISSUE 04

Hobbies

One of the main reasons people have hobbies is to kill* time. In the modern world, many of the great developments in science and technology have given us all a lot of spare* time. But few of us use our extra time creatively, so we get bored*. Therefore, we need a hobby to make the time pass enjoyably: We collect stamps or learn how to cook or just listen to music.

One of the problems, though, is having expensive hobbies. Usually these are intended to show off* our wealth or to demonstrate that we are up-to-date* with some supposed* trend, rather than supporting any genuine* interest we have in them. Too often, we can't really afford them; but even if we can, they just feed* our general discontent because we spend so much money without relieving* our boredom.

kill : spend time doing (sth) **spare :** available to be used
get bored : tired and annoyed by uninteresting things **show off :** make (sth) very noticeable
up-to-date : modern or fashionable **supposed :** claimed to be true or real
genuine : actual, real, or true **feed :** give support or strength **relieve :** reduce or remove (sth)

Comprehension

1. What are two reasons given for having a hobby?
2. Why are hobbies necessary in the modern world?
3. What is wrong with having expensive hobbies?

Express  Yourself

1. What hobbies do you have?
2. Do you have enough time to indulge* them? Why or why not?
3. How much do your hobbies cost you?
4. With whom do you spend time enjoying your hobbies?
5. Do you make friends with people who have the same pursuits*?
6. What are the best things you like about your hobbies?
7. Are there any hobbies you have given up*? Why?
8. What hobbies would you like to try soon?
9. Did you ever recommend that family members share your entertainment* with you?
10. Some say "shopping is my hobby." What do you think of that opinion?
11. What are some expensive hobbies? What are some cheap ones? Are the expensive ones better than the others?
12. What are the most addictive hobbies, do you think?
13. There are said to be five "deadly" hobbies for men—cars, audio systems, golf clubs, watches, and cameras. Why are they dangerous? Are they only for men? What are the deadly hobbies for women?
14. Have you ever seen any people who have very strange hobbies?
15. Some say, "My job is my hobby," and vice versa*. What do you think of this idea? Do you think these people are happy?

---

indulge : do the things you want to do
pursuit : activity done for pleasure
give up : stop an activity or effort
entertainment : amusement or pleasure
vice versa : the other way around

Opinion Samples

1. My sisters say shopping is their hobby, but I disagree with them — it is an addiction. They go shopping every day, no matter what other obligations* they may have. They spend hours looking at stuff, holding it, discussing it, and putting it on, even if they have no interest in buying it. But they never come home empty-handed — they always have to buy something, whether they need it or not, and once they get it home, they promptly* forget about it.

2. I have two hobbies. One costs a lot of money, and the other one hardly costs anything. The expensive one is photography. The camera itself was very costly, but I am constantly updating it with new bags, filters, lenses, lights, tripods*, and so forth, and of course I need more than one camera! In addition, I buy a lot of photography books and magazines. I still have a darkroom, and I enjoy occasionally developing* my own film, but at least that's one expense that is optional these days. My other hobby is taking long walks. All I need is a good pair of shoes — and it gives me an excuse* to take a camera along.

Dialog

The Joys of Hunting

Helen : I can't understand you sometimes. You constantly lecture* me about needing to economize*, but every chance you get, you go on a hunting trip with your buddies. That costs a lot more than anything I spend money on.

Charles: You just don't understand. We've been doing this for years. It's our one shared activity that bonds* us together.

Helen : You're right — I don't understand. Part of your hunting trip involves consuming lots of alcohol, right?

Charles: Sure. Of course. But not while we're actually hunting — that would be dangerous.

Helen : But you can drink closer to home. You all do anyhow.

Charles: But it's just not the same. Drinking on a hunting trip is a ceremony celebrating our manhood*, but drinking after work is just a form of relaxation. There's no comparison.

---

obligation : (sth) you must do **promptly :** without delay **tripod :** stand for a camera
develop : make a photograph from film **excuse :** (false) reason **lecture :** talk seriously or reprovingly to (sb)
economize : use money carefully **bond :** establish a relationship with (sb)
manhood : qualities such as strength and courage that are expected in a man

Helen : You complain if your bed is a little lumpy*, but you don't mind sleeping in a tent on the hard, cold ground.

Charles: You're right. But camping out is part of the ritual*. And sometimes we rent a cabin instead.

Helen : More expense! For a crude*, cold, uncomfortable room!

Charles: It's the fact that we are out in nature instead of being cooped up* in the city that's so meaningful. It's like living the way our ancestors did hundreds of years ago!

Helen : Most of the time you don't even bag* any game*.

Charles: The enjoyment is in the process, not the product. Getting meat at the end of it is a bonus, but the hunt itself is the real purpose.

Helen : If you do get lucky, you have to do all the disgusting, bloody cleaning and skinning of the animal before you can bring the meat home. I can't even get you to wash the dishes here!

Charles: My hunting partners never nag me, either. We all pitch in* and do our share of the chores, and we feel very equal to each other despite the separation according to social rank once we come back home.

Helen : I'm all for* equality. So I'll make you a proposition. Every time you go out on a hunting expedition*, I get to take a shopping spree* trip with my friends, in Paris, or Singapore, or Rome, or wherever we want to go. That way we can both enjoy our favorite hobby!

– What gives you the right to steal my trophy? I killed it, you didn't.
– Exactly. The moral responsibility for ending a life is yours. I'm doing the responsible thing by removing the dead carcass*.
– But the hunter has rights.
– So does the deer.

QUESTIONS

1. Have you ever gone hunting? Or taken a fishing trip? Or camped out? Describe your experience.
2. Does Charles' explanation sound appealing to you? Would you like to join him sometime? Why or why not?
3. Define "hobby." Can anything be a hobby?

---

lumpy : having lumps; being not smooth **ritual** : acts or ceremonies performed in the same way
crude : very simple and basic **coop (sb) up** : make (sb) stay indoors or in a small space
bag : kill or catch animals **game** : wild animal hunted for food **pitch in** : add your help
all for : completely in favor of **expedition** : long and carefully organized trip
spree : short period of time when you do a lot of (sth) **carcass** : body of a dead animal

Read & Discuss

Is Golf a Hobby or Just Business?

Golf has become a prominent* part of doing business. It provides an opportunity to spend a lot of intimate time together, to develop a personal relationship, and to discuss a deal* in an informal manner. In some situations, membership in a country club is considered to be a legitimate* business expense that can be written off from taxes. However, even though ambitious businessmen may take up the sport for practical reasons, they often come to love it as a sport in its own right*. Playing golf is a notoriously* difficult process, full of unexpected obstacles and frustrations. It requires skill, patience, and a great deal of determination. Most golfers say they are not playing against someone else, only against themselves, and they find it a challenging* endeavor*. It also provides an opportunity both to get some good exercise and to spend some time in the fresh air, surrounded by green grass, water, and trees. So, many executives continue to play the game even after they retire from business.

– I play golf whenever I can. I love the sport.
– I care nothing for the game, but it's a great business opportunity.
– Maybe I'm obsessed, but when I see the sun in the sky, it reminds me of a golf ball.
– You're crazy. It reminds me of a big golden coin.

QUESTIONS

1. Do you golf? How often? If so, why? If not, would you like to?
2. What is your favorite sport? Do you play or just watch?
3. Can golf be played cheaply, or is it always an expensive hobby?

---

prominent : important and well-known deal : agreement or arrangement in business
legitimate : allowed according to rules or laws in its own right : because of its own special qualities
notorious : known widely challenging : difficult
endeavor : serious effort or attempt

Let's Talk Funny

Underage Drinking Soars*

Adult: You kids drink too much and it will lead to* trouble.

Teen: We're just following the habits we learn from adults. We're not to blame*.

Adult: Don't blame us! Haven't we always told you, "Do as we say, not as we do"?

QUESTIONS

1. Who is to blame for bad behavior, the role model or the performer?
2. Are the warnings against drinking exaggerated*, in your opinion?
3. Which is worse, drinking alcohol or smoking cigarettes?

---

soar : increase quickly to a high level **lead to (sth) :** result in (sth)
to blame : responsible for (sth) bad **on the rocks :** with ice but with no water added
monkey see, monkey do : people will often do what they see other people doing
exaggerate : describe (sth) as larger or greater than it really is

Points to Ponder

1

Finding a simple life is today's most complicated job.

2

Why not learn to enjoy the little things—there are so many of them.

3

What we enjoy, not what we have, constitutes* our abundance*.

4

A lot of singers on TV are worth watching. Too bad they're not worth listening to.

---

constitute : make up or form (sth)
abundance : plentifulness of the good things of life

The following sentences are all related thematically. They express a wide difference of opinions and attitudes. You may agree with some of them and disagree with others. Please discuss what you think the sentences mean and what you think about them.

5

Hobbies of any kind are boring except to people who have the same hobby.

6

Beware the hobby that eats*.

7

Nothing grows faster than a fish from the time he bites until he gets away*.

8

I did nothing but work. I made work my hobby. I was lucky that way.

---

eat : consume, esp. money
get away : avoid being caught; escape

1

Fishing is hard work, since it depends on the actions of the fish, not the fisherman. Why don't they bite?

I thought I was hungry until I heard his phone.

I guess that's why fish haven't become slaves to smart phones.

I guess human schools don't teach values.

It's a good thing for us that he doesn't know he can't live a simple life at the same time as a complicated, modern one.

What's wrong with him? We learned that in school.

2

I can enjoy a symphony without attending a concert. I can appreciate a good book without having to go to an expensive university. I don't have to own an orchard to be able to eat a delicious apple.

3
Do you like my new sports car? I paid big bucks for it!
But my second-hand dirt bike gives me freedom and pleasure. I don't have monthly payments, and I don't have to stay on the road.

4
I'd like to thank our beautiful guest. But I miss the days of silent films.
Fortunately for my fans, who admire the way I look, we don't have silent television.

5

rags : old or tattered clothes **knock off :** stop doing (sth) such as work **bum :** tramp; vagrant
strike it rich : become rich suddenly

6

7

That fish must have weighed four kilos! But the only ones I ever catch are so small that I have to throw them back.

8

- You're the happiest bartender I've ever seen.
- I enjoy my occupation. It's the only job I've ever had that let me drink on the job. What do you do?
- I'm a wine taster.
- Really? I'm envious.
- No, you don't understand. I'm only allowed to taste, but never to swallow.

ISSUE 05

Vacation

As people make more money, they may think that now is the time to enjoy themselves more. Leisure becomes more important in their lives. As their psychological horizons* expand beyond just earning an income, they also want to find out more about the world, so they want to travel. One problem, however, is that they don't really know where they want to go or what they want to do when they get there. In that case, they blindly* go somewhere just because they think it is fashionable to do so. Often they take some package tour that offers them "10 countries in 7 days." That way, they collect a lot of stamps in their passports and a lot of predictable photographs, but they don't have much fun or relaxation, and they don't really know very much about where they've been. A much better approach for knowledgeable* tourism would be to decide where they really want to go, and why, and then plan far enough in advance in order to accomplish those goals. That way the vacation is both more enjoyable and more affordable*.

– Where are you now?
– I'm taking a nice hike on a beautiful mountain trail. What are you doing?
– I'm here at the beach, relaxing and having a good time.
– I wish I was there with you, but I can't stand* the hot sun.
– That's all right. I don't want to spend all day tramping* through the woods. Have fun.
– Next year we should plan a vacation we'd both enjoy together.
– Great! How about shopping?
– Hmm... How about bear hunting?

---

horizons : limits of your ideas, knowledge, and experience
blindly : without thinking or questioning
knowledgeable : intelligent and well-informed
affordable : not too expensive
stand : be willing or able to accept (sb/sth) unpleasant
tramp : walk for a long distance or time

Comprehension

1. Why has travel become more popular?
2. What mistakes do people sometimes make?
3. What should they do to make the most* of their vacations?

Express  Yourself

1. How much paid vacation do you get each year? Is it enough?
2. What do you think is the best season for vacationing?
3. What was your best vacation trip? And your worst one? Describe them.
4. What's on your next summer bucket list*?
5. Do you know how to save traveling expenses, especially when you go abroad? What tips* can you share?
6. When you travel in foreign countries, do you easily adapt* to new surroundings, including the native food, or do you have trouble adjusting*?
7. Do you like to backpack*?
8. Some people enjoy vacations in their hometown, avoiding heavy traffic as well as overcrowding. What do you think of this approach?
9. Would you be willing to sacrifice some vacation time for better pay, or vice versa?
10. People say traveling together causes friends to become estranged*. Do you have any explanation for that?
11. What have you learned from travel?

make the most of (sth) : use (sth) in a way that will get the best result
bucket list : list of things (sb) wants to achieve or experience, as before reaching a certain age or dying
tip : piece of advice or useful information
adapt to : become adjusted to new conditions
adjust : become used to a new situation
backpack : hike or travel with a backpack
estranged : no longer close or affectionate to (sb)

Opinion Samples

1. Right now I have a growing family, and expenses are really piling up* to pay for doctors and teachers, as well as the necessity of buying a bigger home. We are financially stretched to the bone*. I really like the idea of having a long, leisurely vacation so I could travel and relax, but it is a low priority* these days. If I had a choice, right now I would rather work all year for extra money to cover my current cost of living; but I'd like to be able to save up* my vacation time and use it in the future, when I can afford to take more time off.

2. When I was in my twenties I bummed around* with some friends for a summer. We backpacked all over Europe and found cheap accommodations*, and we had a lot of fun. Our friendship got even stronger as a result. But last year one of those same old friends and I went on a trip together. It was a spur-of-the-moment* sort of thing, but we both had some time off at the same time, and we thought it would be a great idea to relive* part of our past. What a mistake that was! We couldn't find anything to do in common that we enjoyed. He wanted to go to a lot more museums than I did, and I wanted to stay out later partying than he did. We quarreled* over where we stayed and where we ate and what we were going to do next. By the end of the week we were barely on speaking terms*. It's a good thing the trip ended when it did, because our friendship probably could not have survived even one more day.

Dialog

How to Have Fun on Your Holiday

Joe : Where do you want to go on vacation this year?

Betty: The beach?

Joe : We went there last year, but we didn't have a very good time. There were too many mosquitoes, and the food was of poor quality.

Betty: And expensive, as I recall.

Joe : The room was not comfortable to sleep in, and the neighbors were too noisy.

---

pile up : increase in amount　financially stretched to the bone : financially overextended
priority : condition of being more important than (sth) else
save up (sth) : accumulate (sth) for a particular purpose　bum around : spend time relaxing
accommodations : place where travelers can sleep and find other services
spur-of-the-moment : done suddenly and without planning
relive : experience (sth) again in your imagination　quarrel : argue about　on speaking terms : speaking

Betty: And all we had to show for our trouble when we got back home was a sunburn.

Joe : So, let's do something else.

Betty: Go abroad?

Joe : I don't think we can afford it this year. We're still paying off the new car. But maybe next year. We can start budgeting* for it.

Betty: Then where shall we go?

Joe : I have an idea! But I don't know if you'll go for* it.

Betty: What is it?

Joe : We can stay home!

Betty: Stay home?

Joe : Sure! It won't cost anything, but we'll have the chance to do things here that we've always wanted to do but didn't have the time.

Betty: And the crowds will be a lot smaller, because most other people will be out of town then.

Joe : We can take our time and do what we want to do. No traffic jams* or crowded subways.

Betty: And we'll also be able to fix up* some things around the house that we've been neglecting.

Joe : So it's settled*, then? We're just going to stay home this vacation?

Betty: Right! We're going to take a "staycation!"

QUESTIONS

1. What did you do for your last vacation? Would you like to do that again?
2. If time and money were not an issue*, describe your ideal vacation.
3. Does the notion of a staycation appeal* to you? Why or why not?

---

budget : plan to spend (an amount of money) for a particular purpose **go for** : accept or agree
traffic jam : long line of vehicles that cannot move along the road, or that can only move very slowly
fix up : improve the appearance or condition of (sth) by repairing it or making changes to it
settled : agreed **issue** : problem **appeal** : seem attractive and interesting

Read & Discuss

What's the Purpose of Traveling?

The more archeologists* find out about the past, the more they realize how much mankind has been on the move. The earliest hunter-gatherer societies were constantly on the go* as they searched for new food supplies. But even after they began planting crops and raising animals to eat, groups of people continued to migrate* in order to find a better place to live. Even in settled societies, merchants had to go abroad to buy and sell their wares, soldiers had to travel to confront their foes and conquer new lands, itinerant* religious leaders felt the need to convert* as many souls as possible, and scholars wanted to expand their own data base by studying foreign cultures. Even long before the modern tourism industry took hold*, humans always showed a restless* geographic spirit.

QUESTIONS

1. What are the main reasons people travel today?
2. Why do some people spend a long time living abroad, not just making brief tours?
3. What reasons do people have for becoming expatriates* or immigrants?

archeologist : scientist who studies ancient societies **on the go :** very active or busy
migrate : go to another area or country **itinerant :** traveling from place to place
convert : persuade (sb) to change from one religion, belief, etc., to another **take hold :** start to have an effect
restless : unable to rest or relax **expatriate :** (sb) who lives in a foreign country

Be Sun-Smart to Prevent Skin Cancer

Man: Be careful when you tan*. It causes skin cancer.

Woman: Don't worry! I always carry sunscreen*.

Man: The chemicals in sunscreen also cause skin trouble.

Woman: Then what should I do?

Man: Just wait. Someone is bound* to invent an artificial sun that doesn't emit* ultraviolet rays.

QUESTIONS

1. Do you always carry sunscreen when you go to the beach or plan on being outdoors for a considerable* time? Why or why not?
2. What do you think about indoor tanning salons? Do you think the government should ban them?
3. Why do you think some people see "dark" skin as being more attractive?
4. In some cultures, a tan is considered a mark of low status. Why would people think so?

---

tan : become brown or browner after exposure to the sun
sunscreen : lotion rubbed onto the skin to protect it from the sun
be bound : be very likely
emit : send out
considerable : large in size, amount, or quantity

Points to Ponder

1

My vacations are easy to plan—my boss tells me when, and my wife tells me where.

2

Vacations are a little like love affairs—anticipated* with relish,* experienced with inconvenience, and remembered with nostalgia.*

3

Summer vacations make kids brown, get mothers in the pink,* and put fathers in the red.*

4

No one needs a vacation more than the person who has just had one.

---

anticipate : expect (sth) with pleasure **relish :** great enjoyment
nostalgia : sentimental longing or wishful affection for the past
in the pink : in extremely good health and spirits
in the red : spending and owing more money than is being earned

The following sentences are all related thematically. They express a wide difference of opinions and attitudes. You may agree with some of them and disagree with others. Please discuss what you think the sentences mean and what you think about them.

5

On vacation, I totally unplug and leave the smart phone at home. But I take along my old-fashioned cell phone and make sure there's a cyber cafe nearby.

6

I've heard that a vacation spot out of season always has a very special magic. But I wouldn't know — I've never actually been to one.

7

The alternative* to taking a vacation is to stay home and tip every third person you see.

8

By and large*, mothers and housewives are the only workers who never have regular time off*.

alternative : one of two or more available possibilities
by and large : in general
time off : time for rest or recreation away from one's work

1

—What a wonderful vacation! Not a care in the world.
—Except for paying for it.
—All you do is complain about money. Relax. Enjoy your life.
—Somebody has to worry about the expense! But I learned my lesson. Next time, I'll pay for a busboy to carry our bags, no matter what it costs.

2

– I'm in such a hurry to be with you. But there are too many red lights.
– Just think of the red lights as indicating anticipation.
– Okay. That's very poetic. And the green lights would be the speed and excitement of the experience.
– Right! But what about the yellow ones?
– Don't pay any attention to them.
– Why not?
– On the way to our rendezvous* they represent caution, a warning to think about what we're about to do.
– Oh. And afterwards?
– A nostalgic memory of a wonderful time in the past.

rendezvous : meeting at an agreed time and place, typically between two people

perk up : become more lively or cheerful

5

When I go on vacation I like to rough it*. So I don't take my smart phone with me. Unfortunately, even if it's unplugged, my cell phone still rings!

rough it : live usually for a short time without the normal things that make life comfortable

6

- I can just imagine how pleasant this beach would be if there weren't so many tourists here.
- You have a good imagination then. All we've ever seen of it is during the peak season.
- Maybe we should come back some time when it's deserted*.
- But the only reason nobody would be here is if it's boring.
- You're right, I suppose. But it's still nice to imagine that it would be both empty and fun for the two of us.

deserted : empty because people have left

7

Maybe I'm too much of a feminist.
I insisted on being first in line.

I'm sick and tired
of always being
in the middle.

Sometimes a dog's life ain't
so bad. I wonder if this tip
is enough to buy a T-bone.

8

I work all day.
When I go home I
have to cook and then
wash the dishes.
Then I always have
laundry to do.
And housework!
I can't forget to feed
and walk the dog. And
where's my husband
all the time?

I'm out with the boys
enjoying myself. But I
appreciate all your hard
work on my behalf.

ISSUE 06

Family

The family is the most fundamental* institution in human society. Indeed, in one form or another, it seems to be one of the commonalities* between many human and nonhuman species as well. Just think about the care a mother cat gives her kittens or the effort that mama birds take to feed their nestlings*. Parenting usually involves more than just the feeding of offspring; teaching and bonding are also all-important*. But one thing that distinguishes* human families from those of other animals are their adaptability*. Family structures vary widely from culture to culture. Some are polygamous*, many are monogamous*, and a few have no or little formal form of marriage at all and regard child rearing as a communal* duty. Even when societies have deeply ingrained* notions of the "normal" family composition, many variations exist due to the vagaries* of human circumstance. So, we have adoptive children, single-parent households, and couples living with children from previous marriages. Sometimes it is a grandmother or uncle who is the primary caregiver; sometimes even young kids have the responsibility for looking after themselves and their younger siblings. Families take many forms, but no matter the actual form it takes, a family of some sort is still the operative* unit in every society in the world.

---

fundamental : relating to the most important part of (sth); basic **commonality :** shared feature or quality
nestling : young bird that is not yet able to fly away from the nest **all-important :** very important
distinguish : make (sb/sth) different or special in some way **adaptability :** ability to change or be changed in order to fit or work in some situation **polygamy :** practice of having more than one husband or wife at the same time **monogamy :** practice of being married to only one person at a time
communal : shared by a group, esp. a group of people living together **ingrained :** firmly established
vagaries : changes that are difficult to predict or control **operative :** most important
assorted : including several kinds

Comprehension

1. What is the "normal" family structure in your culture? How common is it nowadays?
2. According to the paragraph, if a mother and father are not the caregivers, who are? Give at least three answers.
3. Why are families necessary? What functions do they possess?

Express  Yourself

1. Who is the boss in your home, you or your spouse? (Be honest!)
2. Who should do the dishes, the husband or the wife? Always?
3. Should wives work outside the home?
4. Should husbands do household chores if their wives have a job? What if they don't have a job?
5. How do you divide household chores among your family members? Is that fair?
6. Should wives work outside the home even after they have children?
7. How should a man feel if his wife makes more money than he does?
8. If a woman makes enough money to support the family, should her husband be allowed to quit his job?
9. What did you do, and how did you feel, when your first child was born?
10. Is having a son as your first child very important to you?
11. Do you enjoy being with your kids?
12. Who should be in charge of disciplining* children?
13. Is raising kids these days easy or difficult? Why?
14. Is your pet treated like a family member?
15. What do you think about living with one's parents-in-law?
16. Is your family usually harmonious or discordant*?
17. What causes trouble within a family?
18. People say poor families live more amicably* than rich ones. Do you think that's true? Why or why not?
19. Kids from poor families may mature* sooner than those from rich ones. Why? Is this a good thing or a bad thing?

---

discipline : train (sb) to obey rules and control their own behavior
discordant : not agreeing; not in harmony
amicable : friendly and pleasant; without serious disagreement
mature : become sensible and start to behave like an adult

Opinion Samples

1. Immediate conditioning* or reinforcement is always more effective than delayed conditioning. So the parent who is closest to the situation should be the one in charge of instilling* discipline. Usually, that is the mother, if she spends most of her time at home. But the other parent also needs to be involved. Not only must he (assuming that the other one is the father) be kept informed, he should also realize that one parent second-guessing* the other, or countermanding* the other's actions, just leads to chaos. If there is no united front, it does not take kids long to figure out how to pit their parents against* each other in order to get their own way. So, no matter who is responsible for discipline, it is imperative* that the process be transparent*, consistent, immediate, and fair.

2. No matter how much we feel we are part of a family, we are also egocentric* individuals. We want to be loved, respected, and paid attention to. When we feel our physical or emotional needs are not being met, we react. This reaction is often impulsive and personal and, many times, triggers* anger and resentment against other family members. The immediate cause of a dispute may seem to be a money issue or an instance of bad behavior, but usually that is just an excuse; it is the underlying* failure to properly stroke each other's ego* that is the real cause. The solution is to communicate honestly and try to be empathetic* towards each other, but this is easier said than done.

Dialog

Is Adoption a Moral Responsibility?

June : Why don't we adopt a child?
Ralph : I haven't ever really thought about it.
June : So, think. Let's do it.
Ralph : Don't rush into* this. Adoption is a tricky* matter. It's expensive and legally complicated.
June : Just because it's not easy should not mean we can't do it.
Ralph : Raising kids is hard under any circumstances, but raising kids that we aren't biologically connected to is particularly difficult. We don't know anything about where they came from or any genetic predispositions* they may have.
June : But these are problems that can all be dealt with through love.

---

conditioning : act of training (sb) to do (sth) or to behave in a certain way in a particular situation
instill : gradually cause (sb) to have an attitude, feeling, etc. **second-guess :** criticize or question the actions or decisions of (sb) **countermand :** cancel (an order), esp. by giving a new order
pit (sb) against (sb) : cause (sb) to fight or compete against another person **imperative :** very important
transparent : easy to notice or understand; obvious **egocentric :** caring too much about yourself; self-centered **trigger :** cause (sth) to start or happen **underlying :** very basic or important
stroke (sb's) ego : flatter (sb) **empathy :** ability to understand and share the feeling of (sb)
rush into (sth) : get involved in (sth) without taking enough time to think carefully about it **tricky :** difficult to deal with **predisposition :** tendency to behave in a particular way or suffer from a particular illness

Ralph : But that's just it*. How can people decide to love someone that they are not connected to? I love our kids, but I know that they are my children; they aren't just strangers.

June : Adopted kids aren't "strangers" either! They're part of a family.

Ralph : Don't you think having more kids would be unfair to the ones we already have? There would be less of everything to go around*. Don't you think this would cause resentment and jealousy?

June : If we've done our parenting job properly, our kids won't feel that way. Everybody in the family needs to love one another, even when it's inconvenient.

Ralph : Why the sudden concern over adoption? You never mentioned it before.

June : I just got to thinking about how fortunate we are to have the great family we do and how unlucky so many kids are not to ever have one. I think we all have a duty to be generous to the disadvantaged, but in this case I think the conscious generosity of the act would cause us to gain even more than the child.

Ralph : If you feel that strongly about it, I'll consider the matter. But I'm not ready to make up my mind yet.

June : We need to talk it through*, I agree, and find out exactly what adoption entails* before we commit ourselves. But I do want to seriously consider the option, not just dismiss the notion out of hand*.

Ralph : We should also get our kids involved in the discussion to see how they feel.

QUESTIONS

1. Do you know anyone who is adopted or has adopted children? What do you know about their situation?
2. What is the strongest point in favor of* adoption? Against* adoption?
3. Some people deliberately adopt kids with severe handicaps or illnesses, or from different racial groups. Discuss your reaction to these people.

---

that's just it : you have identified the exact issue that must be dealt with **go around :** share with each other
talk (sth) through : discuss (sth) with (sb) in order to make a decision or reach an agreement
entail : involve (sth) as a necessary or inevitable part **out of hand :** very quickly without serious thought
in favor of : approving of **against :** in opposition to

Read & Discuss

The Generation Gap Never Narrows

Our parents and their generation grew up a long time ago. The social situation was different then. Technology, in particular, has altered* the way we communicate and perhaps even the way we think. Based on their own experiences, our parents have developed a certain set of attitudes and objectives* which make sense to them. But they may not be particularly relevant* to us. We have our own situation to deal with, and we need to discover our own identities* and make our own way in the world, which may not be the same fate our parents would choose for us or even be comfortable with. So there is a gap between our own expectations and those of the older generation, and we both need to be sympathetic* toward each other. We also need to realize that a similar gap will exist between us and the generation that succeeds* us. It is a never-changing process.

QUESTIONS

1. What is the biggest difference between you and your parents?
2. In terms of attitude, what is the most important area of progress that your generation has made?
3. What do you think about the direction the younger generation is heading in*?

---

alter : change objective : (sth) you are trying to achieve; goal or purpose
relevant : appropriate identity : qualities, beliefs, etc. that make (sb) different from others
sympathetic : showing support for or approval of (sth) succeed : come after
out-of-date : not useful, correct, or fashionable anymore head in : move in a specified direction

When Roles Reverse: The Rise of the Stay-at-Home Husband

Man: I resigned last month and became a househusband.

Friend: Really? How is it?

Man: I enjoy it very much. I have no boss complaining about me, and my work schedule is flexible*. I can tell my kids what to do and get pocket money from my wife. Isn't that a wonderful situation?

Friend: I guess so, but what if your wife fires you?

Man: Then I can collect alimony*.

QUESTIONS

1. Is there any difference between being a housewife and being a househusband?
2. Do you think many men are suited to the role?
3. Should alimony be gender-neutral? Is it appropriate in every case?

flexible : easily changed
alimony : money that a court orders (sb) to pay regularly to a former wife or husband after a divorce
scapegoat : blame (sb) publicly for (sth) bad that has happened, even though it was not their fault
see fit : deem appropriate

Points to Ponder

1

There is just as much authority* in the family today as there ever was —only now the children exercise* it.

2

Can you remember when the family meals were carefully thought out instead of being thawed* out?

3

Don't confuse the people who are always around with those who are always there.

4

Nowadays there are more model homes than model families.

authority : power to give orders or make decisions
exercise : use (an ability, power, etc.)
thaw : make (sth) warm enough to become liquid or soft

The following sentences are all related thematically. They express a wide difference of opinions and attitudes. You may agree with some of them and disagree with others. Please discuss what you think the sentences mean and what you think about them.

5

In today's inflation, a big spender is any man who can support his family.

6

There is no cure for laziness in a man, except a nagging* wife and needy* kids.

7

It takes a raft* of money to keep the family afloat* these days.

8

Domestic tranquility* is a luxury you can enjoy only between the children's bedtime and your own.

nag : annoy (sb) with repeated questions, requests, or orders
needy : needing a lot of attention, affection, or emotional support
raft : large amount of (sth)   afloat : able to continue without suffering financial failure
tranquility : state of being quiet and peaceful

1

2

Have you ever wondered what it would be like to live like a family again? Spend time talking to each other while preparing a delicious meal? Taste the savory* flavor of a well-cooked roast? Now you can! Throw out that old microwave. Get the new flame broiler for your kitchen. Light up* every meal! The natural way. (Batteries not included. In fact, there are no batteries!)

savory : having a pleasant and attractive smell or taste
light up : begin to burn

treat : pay for (sb's) food, drink, or entertainment

5

It's hard work to carry the family load, but I try to lift us as far as I can.
I miss our big house.
Me, too, but I think we're all a lot closer to each other now.

6

You've slept long enough. It's Saturday, and you've got lots of household chores to do.
I have to have a new dress for a party.
Daddy, Daddy! Get up! I need my allowance.
Weekends at home are a lot more stressful than weekdays at work. Even though my job is in Traffic Control.

7

bail out : leave or escape a harmful or difficult situation **waterlogged :** filled or soaked with water

8

castaway : (sb) who is left alone in a place (such as an island) as a result of a storm, shipwreck, etc.
turn up : be found, usually unexpectedly

ISSUE 07

Friends

Like most people, I have a lot of acquaintances* but very few friends. In the first category are people I have worked with for years, old school chums*, neighbors, and colleagues* in various organizations. We are generally friendly and polite toward each other, we exchange pleasantries* and chitchat*, and we even eat out together and invite each other to parties, and so forth. Nevertheless, even though we know each other very well indeed, we remain acquaintances rather than friends. To me, friendship is a sacred* obligation as deep, unquestioning*, and unalterable as love. Friends are willing to aid and protect each other under any circumstance, despite whatever sacrifice may be required. They may quarrel at times, but the relationship between them is a part of their very being. Obviously, no one can survive* the demands of an unlimited number of true friends, but it is a poor life indeed that does not have at least one such true friend. In this case, the quantity is far less important than the quality.

---

acquaintance : (sb) you know, but who is not a close friend
chum : close friend   colleague : (sb) who works with you
pleasantries : things (such as greetings) that people say in order to be polite
chitchat : friendly conversation about things that are not very important
sacred : highly valued and important   unquestioning : certain and without doubts
survive : endure or live through

Comprehension

1. What is the difference between friends and acquaintances?
2. What other human association is friendship akin to*?
3. Why can't we be expected to survive the demands of an unlimited number of true friends?

Express  Yourself

1. Why do we need friends?
2. How do you usually make friends with other people?
3. How did you meet your best friend?
4. What do you think matters most when making friends?
5. What usually causes trouble between friends?
6. Do you meet your friends socially very often? What do you usually do together?
7. Do you tell your friends everything about your private life?
8. What's the difference between having male and female friends?
9. What's the difference between the friends you have made in elementary, middle, and high school, college, and at the workplace?
10. Do you ever feel disappointed with your friends? Under what circumstances?
11. Which is stronger, love or friendship?
12. What is the most important thing in maintaining a harmonious friendship?
13. Do you believe in the saying, "Out of sight, out of mind"?
14. What is the difference between a true friend and a false friend?
15. Some people say they prefer "shallow" friendships instead of deep ones because they have been betrayed a lot. What do you think of their attitude?
16. Some people say, "Pets are my real friends. They never disappoint me under any circumstances. They're always loyal to me." Does this idea make sense? If not, what is wrong with it?

---

akin to : very similar to (sth)

Opinion Samples

1. Being alone in the universe is simply an intolerable* condition. No one is self-sufficient, no matter how smart, rich, or talented. We are all social animals, even the most solitary among us. We have to share our existence with others, even to the point that if we absolutely cannot form effective human bonds, we cultivate* strong attachments to pets or even inanimate* objects. So, we need "friends" in order to live with ourselves.

2. A false friend displays a smile and honeyed* words, but the smile is for appearance's sake only, and the words are never accompanied by action. A false friend needs you more than he or she will ever allow you to rely on him or her; it is a one-way street, but it is never Your Way. On the other hand, a true friend may not always be outwardly friendly but is always honest; and he or she will always provide you with any assistance you need without ever expecting anything in return except your own unwavering* loyalty.

Dialog

The Friendship Between a Man and a Woman

Ralph : I'm going out to meet my friends, but I won't be out late.

Honey: Every weekend it's the same thing. You meet your friends, but you abandon* me.

Ralph : You're welcome to come too.

Honey: But I don't fit in*. They aren't my friends, and I'd just get in the way* of your enjoyment.

Ralph : But they could be your friends, if you'd just give them a chance.

Honey: No. They're men. They can never be my friends.

Ralph : Don't be silly. Friendship can be cross-gender*, you know.

Honey: No, it can't. Men and women are too different psychologically. Expectations are different.

Ralph : I don't think so.

Honey: But it's true! Women always want to share their innermost* feelings with one

---

intolerable : too bad, harsh, or severe to be accepted or tolerated
cultivate : improve or develop (sth) by careful attention inanimate : not living
honeyed : soothing, soft, and intended to please or flatter
unwavering : continuing in a strong and steady way abandon : leave and never return
fit in : belong in a particular situation, place, or group in the way : in a position to obstruct, hinder, or interfere
cross-gender : not restricted to a single sex innermost : most private and personal

another, but men never do. With men, all talk is superficial, about sports or politics or news events, but it's never personal. They avoid talking about their hopes and fears, but that's all women ever want to discuss. And, of course, how other women stack up* in terms of their desirability in men's eyes.

Ralph : Oh, you're just putting men and women into stereotypical* boxes. At heart, men and women are all human beings, with the same needs and emotions.

Honey: There are individual variations*, of course, but in general what I said is true. I've listened to men talk to one another, I've seen them interact with each other, and most are just too afraid or too reticent* to talk about themselves, and the other men get uncomfortable if one of their male companions gets too personal.

Ralph : Men talk about themselves all the time.

Honey: Not really. They talk about their sexual conquests or about their possessions or their business success. They talk about THINGS, but not about themselves. Women talk about the same things, too, but they also spend a lot more time discussing their feelings, even their most private ones.

Ralph : Okay, I agree that men and women communicate differently, but that doesn't mean they can't be friends. I have female friends, as well as male friends. In fact, some of my best friends are women.

Honey: If you say so*. But I've never had any male friends. And every time I've started to develop a close friendship with a male, it has always turned into a sexual relationship. Or, at least in the man's eyes it became all about sex. If it didn't become physically sexual soon enough, it didn't take long before we stopped seeing each other.

– Sally, I know we can be best friends.
– Harry, I don't think so. You're too handsome to be "just friends" with any woman.
– What if I had reverse plastic surgery? Could we be friends then?
– Why do you think so? I'm only interested in your good looks.

QUESTIONS

1. Are men and women really so different? Discuss your views on this matter.
2. Among your circle of friends from the opposite gender, do you behave the same way as you do with your friends of the same gender? If there are any differences, explain them.
3. Women sometimes develop closer friendships with homosexual men than with heterosexual ones. Why might this be true?

---

stack up : compare **stereotype :** often unfair and untrue belief that many people have about all people or things **variation :** (sth) that is similar to (sth) else but different in some way **reticent :** not willing to tell people about things **if you say so :** expression that shows insincere agreement, used when a speaker doesn't agree with (sb) but doesn't want to argue

Read & Discuss

Friendship & Money

One of my oldest friends contacted me. With tears in his eyes, he told me that he needed an expensive operation right away, but he didn't have enough money to pay for it. Could I help him, he asked. I told him I would have to think about it and then asked him a question in turn: Why didn't he have health insurance? Then he wouldn't have to worry about a medical emergency like this. He just shrugged his shoulders* and had no reply.

After thinking the matter over, I decided what to do. Friendship can only stretch* so far! As a responsible human being, I have obligations that I must honor, especially on behalf of my family; most of my income goes for necessities such as rent, food, clothing, education, and, yes, insurance. If I have money left after that, I will certainly consider helping my friend out, but my share of the cost would have to be pretty modest*. I have often heard that money can break friendships, but I always thought that applied to circumstances when a debt was never repaid. But it can also apply to this situation, in which my friend may never forgive me for not being more generous.

– I don't need a life preserver*. If I have enough money I can hire someone to keep me safe.

– But it's my money! I found it after everyone else jumped ship.

– Even the rats have jumped overboard*, and yet, here you still are! You're so stubbornly greedy.

– If I sink, you're going with me!

QUESTIONS

1. If your friend were sick and needed an expensive operation urgently, would you be willing to give him (or her) the money?
2. Oil and water do not mix; what about money and friendship?
3. Rank in importance these four things and then explain your rationale*: money, family, friendship, and self.

---

shrug (one's) shoulders : raise and then lower your shoulders in order to show that you do not know (sth) or do not care about (sth) **stretch :** continue over a period of time **modest :** not very large in size or amount
life preserver : floating device that is designed to save you from drowning
overboard : over the side of a ship into the water **rationale :** reason or explanation for (sth)

Are You a Bore?

Man: Are you a bore?

Woman: No, I'm not.

Man: Then why do I feel bored when I'm with you?

Woman: Because you are the bore.

Man: No way! I'm never bored when I'm alone.

Woman: A bore is never bored with himself.

QUESTIONS

1. To make friends, does one need to be an entertainer? Can't boring people have friends too?
2. What subjects are the most boring ones to listen to?
3. Do you know anyone who is NEVER boring? Anyone who is ALWAYS boring? Explain your answers.

Points to Ponder

1

Good looks fade*. But a good heart keeps one beautiful forever.

2

Friendship is like money, easier made than kept.

3

Don't fear the enemy who attacks you, but beware* the fake friend who hugs you.

4

Time separates the best friends, but so does money—and marriage.

---

fade : lose strength or freshness
beware : be careful

The following sentences are all related thematically. They express a wide difference of opinions and attitudes. You may agree with some of them and disagree with others. Please discuss what you think the sentences mean and what you think about them.

5

A friend that isn't in need is a friend indeed.

6

The best recipe* for making friends is to be one yourself.

7

Having money and friends is easy. Having friends and no money is an accomplishment.

8

You can win more friends with your ears than with your mouth. But for losing friends, your mouth can be helpful indeed.

---

recipe : way of doing (sth) that will produce a particular result

1
I'm glad I'm not looking in a mirror.
On the contrary, you're still a beautiful woman on the inside.

2
I think good friends should be willing to share everything.
I think good friends should not try to take advantage of each other.

3

give (sb) a lift : make (sb) feel more cheerful and hopeful

4

friendship (n): close, positive relationship that endures forever (until the circumstances of life intervene* such as time, distance, money, marriage, politics, status, jealousy, argumentation*, and neglect.)

intervene : become involved in (sth) in order to have an influence on what happens
argumentation : act of giving reasons for or against (sth)

5

– I'll be with you in a minute. Just as soon as I land this fish.

– I don't have a minute. I need your assistance now.

6

I like spending time together like this. I feel closer to you than when we're dancing.

That's because we are both doing something we enjoy.

7

– Hey, Joe. I like that new car.
– Me, too. We should get together for dinner some time later.
– Sure thing! Next time, it's your turn to pay.
– Of course. You treated me last time.

– Well, Bill, it sure is a nice day.
– It sure is. Would you care for some fish scraps* to go with your burger leftovers?
– Sounds wonderful! Help yourself.

scraps : bits of uneaten food left after a meal

8

We have two ears and just one mouth, so we should listen twice as much as we talk.

ISSUE 08

Jobs

Most people in modern society spend more than eight hours a day working. For many, smart phones and other devices, instead of making their tasks easier, have served to blur* the distinction between "at home" and "on the job." An interesting fact is that bosses often envy the employees, and vice versa*, since people tend to exaggerate* the benefits they don't have and underestimate those that are exclusively* theirs.

Executives* seem to have greater job satisfaction than ordinary workers. After all, they have the power to decide things by themselves, and this can be a very intoxicating* situation. That's why ordinary workers are envious of them. But businessmen must take responsibility for their decisions, and if something goes wrong they may face serious consequences.

Employees, on the other hand, have clearly defined, fairly routine, tasks to perform, but if they do what is expected, they are usually exempt* from any bad consequences. So they have stable positions. A competent worker may enjoy many promotions and raises* but still not have much input into decision making.

Who is happier is not the question. The important thing is that people must evaluate* themselves honestly and decide which category they should belong in — employer or employee.

blur : make (sth) unclear or less distinct **vice versa :** with the order or meaning reversed
exaggerate : describe (sth) as larger or greater than it really is
exclusive : not shared; available to only one person or group
executive : (sb) who manages or directs other people in a company or organization
intoxicating : exhilarating or exciting **exempt :** free from an obligation or liability imposed on others
raise : increase in the amount of your pay
evaluate : judge the value or condition of (sb/sth) in a careful and thoughtful way
credit : approval or praise for doing (sth) good

Comprehension

1. What advantage does a businessperson have?
2. What advantage do workers have?
3. Which is better for you, being an employer or employee?

Express  Yourself

1. Do you think everybody needs a job? Why or why not?
2. Do you like your current job? Why or why not?
3. Would you want your children to do your job?
4. What are your priorities for a suitable job?
5. Would you take a night-shift job if it paid better?
6. Do you have any plans to start your own business?
7. What are some obstacles to starting one's own business?
8. Do you think one's college major determines what one's job will be?
9. Is the relationship between you and your boss good? Why or why not?
10. What does "job" mean to you? Is it only a means of making money?
11. What determines a good or a bad job?
12. What are the best and worst aspects of your job?
13. Do you ever feel like changing jobs? What are the factors you should consider?
14. Our society doesn't seem to be capable enough of accommodating all new college graduates with jobs. What are some useful majors for finding jobs? What are the least useful majors for finding a job?
15. What do you think are the most ideal jobs? What are the worst ones?
16. If you were rich enough to support yourself for the rest of your life, would you choose not to have a job? Or would you search for a job in spite of your wealth?
17. List some jobs that are destined to disappear in a generation. Then list some jobs that are likely to be created in the near future.

More Talking Points

Talk about the good and bad aspects about the following jobs:

a. physician
b. teacher
c. politician
d. head of state
e. farmer
f. pro athlete
g. soldier
h. movie star
i. comedian
j. housewife
k. househusband
l. artist
m. cab driver
n. miner
o. consultant
p. salesperson
q. priest or nun
r. lawyer
s. panhandler

Opinion Samples

1. One of the great myths is that everyone needs a job. Some people are wealthy enough that they don't need to work and can live very well indeed on investment income. Not only the wealthy fit into that category, however; even people of modest means can be very comfortable without a job if they abandon* many of their materialistic desires. Some people genuinely are too physically or emotionally handicapped to be able to work. Some folks have the ability to gain financial support from others without ever having a job. However, even beyond the matter of financial necessity, most people are defined by their occupations, and they find it difficult to fit into society unless they have some sort of job.

2. The two basic requirements for a good job are that it provides a suitable income and reasonable satisfaction in its performance. An old friend of mine was a successful dentist, but he did not have a very high opinion of the profession; he regarded himself as being akin to an oral mechanic. He much preferred being an English teacher, because he enjoyed the interaction with his students and the idea that he was enabling others to improve themselves. But the income disparity* was too great, and he went back to dentistry. However, he was never happy with that decision and eventually just decided to stop eating and drank himself to death.

Dialog

Work Marriage

Beulah : Are you going to be home tonight?

Eugene : It doesn't look like it. I think Harriet and I are going to have to stay in the office late working on a project together.

Beulah : "Working on a project together"? You're sure this is going to be in the office?

Eugene : Of course. Mostly. We'll go someplace to get something to eat. But, otherwise, we'll be in the office until pretty late. I'll call you when I have a better grasp* of the situation.

Beulah : Why can't you come home and eat? Or we could meet someplace?

Eugene : We could meet, but right now I don't know precisely what time that would be feasible*. I won't know until I actually get into the project itself. It probably won't work out* where we could actually get together. But, who knows? Maybe I'll even be able to come home early after all!

---

abandon : give up (sth) completely
disparity : noticeable and often unfair difference between people or things　grasp : understanding of (sth)
feasible : possible to do　work out : happen, develop, or end in a particular way

Beulah : Not likely, though, is it?
Eugene : No. Not likely.
Beulah : You're never home!
Eugene : Not as much as I'd like to be, but it isn't fair to say I'm "never" home.
Beulah : I can't count on* you to be here even on weekends.
Eugene : I'm here most weekends.
Beulah : When you're not on a "business trip" with Harriet!
Eugene : I can't help it that my job requires a lot of travel and late nights. Would you prefer that I be a househusband instead? Then I'd be home all the time. And we'd be broke.
Beulah : I'm not complaining about your job. I'm complaining about your relationship with that woman!
Eugene : It's purely business. But I'm fortunate that I spend so much time with someone like her, instead of someone I can't get along well with.
Beulah : Like me, you mean?
Eugene : Of course not. I love you.
Beulah : You have a funny way of showing it.
Eugene : I can't help it. But there's nothing going on between Harriet and me. We work together. We're close friends. That's all!
Beulah : I used to believe that. But for years you've spent a lot more time with her than you have with me. Gone out of town with her a lot more often than with me.
Eugene : I'm sorry. I'll try to do better.
Beulah : Why don't you just marry her instead? And then you could work on your "projects together" at home, or anywhere you want!
Eugene : That's not fair! You know Harriet is married.
Beulah : Marriage is so inconvenient for you both, isn't it?

QUESTIONS

1. What do you think Beulah means by "working on a project together"?
2. In terms of the dialogue, do you have any advice to Eugene or Beulah about their responses?
3. What do you think about the phenomenon called "work marriage"?

count on : expect (sb) to do (sth) harried : very worried or anxious frumpy : dressed in an unattractive way
on one's behalf : for (sb's) benefit

Read & Discuss

Does a Glass Ceiling* Exist for Women in Our Society?

Way back in 1984 Gay Bryant coined* the term glass ceiling. "Women have reached a certain point," she claimed. "They're in the top of middle management and they're stopping and getting stuck." They were within reach of higher management positions, but some invisible barrier* seemed to block any further progress. Clearly, matters have changed over the last decades — or have they? While we live in a world that is full of women occupying the very highest corporate and political positions, they are still the exception rather than the rule*. Most women still complain that, regardless of their ability and dedication, they will never be able to advance beyond a certain invisible, undefined point. And, meanwhile, they will continue to get paid less than their male colleagues who have the same jobs.

QUESTIONS

1. Does the "glass ceiling" concept only refer to gender discrimination? Can there be a glass ceiling for people based on where they were born or what school they attended or some other arbitrary* status?
2. Is it possible that the glass ceiling is not a genuine phenomenon but merely an excuse people make to rationalize* their own failure to advance? Discuss this notion.
3. What steps should be taken to remove any glass ceiling that may exist?

---

glass ceiling : unofficially acknowledged barrier to advancement in a profession, esp. affecting women and members of minorities
coin : create (a new word or phrase) barrier : (sth) that prevents progress or success
rule : normal or customary state of things
arbitrary : based on random choice or personal whim, rather than any reason or system
rationalize : find or invent a reasonable explanation for your behavior or attitudes

Let's Talk Funny

Consumers Not Spending Like Drunken Sailors*

Man: Super Store is handing out* beer to customers at the front door, hoping they spend more money. And Good Better Best has free whiskey parties for its customers. So what can online stores do to compete?

Friend: They are already aware of the problem. eBuy just announced an additional 20% off to any shoppers who can prove they are shopaholics.

QUESTIONS

1. What is the sales strategy* pursued by Super Store and Good Better Best?
2. What is the alternative sales strategy of eBuy?
3. Which strategy do you think is likely to be more successful?

---

spending like drunken sailors : spending money wildly without thinking
hand out : give (sth) to (sb)
strategy : careful plan or method for achieving a particular goal, usually over a long period of time

Points to Ponder

1

If you think your boss is stupid, remember: You wouldn't have a job if he were any smarter.

2

You can tell a man's character by whether he turns up his nose or his sleeves when offered a job.

3

Going to college won't guarantee you a job, but it'll give you four extra years to worry about getting one.

4

If you think it's expensive to hire a professional to do the job, wait until you hire an amateur.

The following sentences are all related thematically. They express a wide difference of opinions and attitudes. You may agree with some of them and disagree with others. Please discuss what you think the sentences mean and what you think about them.

5

There may be luck in getting a job, but there's none whatsoever involved in keeping it.

6

According to the latest statistics, five million people in our country aren't working. And there are even more if one counts people with desk jobs.

7

I never dreamed about success. I worked for it.

8

Your dream job does not exist. You must create it.

supervise : watch and direct (sb)

look out for : take watchful care of ; be concerned about

in a jiffy : in a moment

5

wither : become dry and weak

6

recharge your batteries : rest and relax in order to regain your energy and strength
tend : give your attention

7

Nobody ever accomplished anything by staying in bed.
Nobody ever succeeded big unless they dreamed big.

8

I know I can win the lottery. I just have to figure out the correct formula.
I hope you succeed. Then you can give me bigger bones.

ISSUE 09

Smoking & Drinking

Despite harsh anti-smoking laws, many people continue to light up*. Around the world, legislators have tried to eradicate* smoking by restricting smoking areas, banning or limiting tobacco ads, imposing steep* taxes, and putting ominous* health warnings on cigarette packages. But the addictive habit is too strong to be ended overnight. The number of young smokers is rapidly growing. Some kids are curious, and others blindly imitate adults or "cool"* role models in the entertainment industry. An even larger portion of young smokers bend* to peer pressure. Another problem is that many governments rely heavily on income generated by cigarette sales, so they are reluctant to crack down* aggressively. They don't seem to realize that skyrocketing health costs will soon outpace* current revenues.

Governments are even less aggressive in their attacks against alcohol. Perhaps this is because of the miserable failure of a famous attempt: In the 1920s the United States prohibited the sale, transport, and manufacture of liquor. The idea was that society would benefit in many ways — not only by removing obvious bad effects associated with drunkenness and alcoholism, including accidents, lost work time, chronic* poverty, and spousal abuse, but also by reducing the incidence of other social evils such as gambling and prostitution (since most of the drinking was in saloons rather than at home). But since many people simply ignored the law and drank anyhow, the main difference was that they had to resort* to expensive, illegal methods of obtaining spirits*. The result was that organized crime grew tremendously rich and powerful. The gangs that profited most also committed many more violent murders, bribed* even more public officials, and sponsored even more casinos and brothels*. After about a decade of Prohibition, the Americans gave up* on the attempt.

---

light up : light a cigarette **eradicate :** remove (sth) completely **steep :** very high
ominous : suggesting that (sth) bad is going to happen **cool :** fashionably attractive or impressive
bend : be forced to submit **crack down :** become more strict in dealing with a problem and punishing the people involved **outpace :** grow faster than (sth) **chronic :** continuing or occurring again and again for a long time **resort to (sth) :** do or use (sth), esp. because no other choices are possible
spirits : strong alcoholic drinks; liquor **bribe :** try to get (sb) to do (sth) by giving or promising (sth) valuable (such as money) **brothel :** building in which prostitutes are available **give up :** stop trying to do (sth)

Comprehension

1. Name three ways governments have tried to control smoking.
2. Why do youngsters usually begin to smoke?
3. What is the problem with the nonaggressive policies most governments follow in regard to smoking?
4. Why did Prohibition fail?

Express  Yourself

1. Do you smoke? Why or why not?
2. Do you ever smoke inside the house?
3. Do you think you could easily quit smoking if you wanted to?
4. Have you tried to quit smoking or drinking? Why or why not?
5. Are you worried about secondhand smoke? What about third-hand smoke*?
6. What do you think about laws that ban smoking in all public places?
7. Do you think cigarettes are expensive enough that smokers are frightened away*?
8. Do you think it fair for non-smokers to be given employment or promotion advantages?
9. If your boy (or girl) friend were a chain smoker*, would you marry him or her?
10. Do you think parents have the right to tell their children to stop smoking?
11. What do you think is the best way to quit smoking?
12. Smokers never seem to worry about smoke-related diseases. Should they? What about the harm they pose to non-smokers?
13. Why is teenage smoking on the rise?
14. What are some good ways to deter* youngsters from touching cigarettes?
15. What would you do if you knew your child smoked?
16. Do you think smoking makes you look cool?
17. What do you think about classifying* tobacco as a toxic substance and treating it like a drug?
18. Do you drink? Why or why not?
19. Some people say they are just social drinkers*. Do you believe them when they tell you that? Why or why not?
20. How often do you drink? Do you think your job "forces" you to drink?
21. What are some personal or social problems associated with drinking?
22. What do you think about making liquor more expensive by raising taxes on it?
23. What are some excuses people make when they fail to quit smoking or drinking?
24. What are good points about smoking or drinking, if there are any?
25. If the government uses scare tactics* to discourage bad habits, such as putting horrifying pictures on cigarette packages, would you be in favor or opposed? Do you think these strategies would be effective?

---

third-hand smoke : odorous residue left on surfaces and clothing from smoking which contains many of the same toxic chemicals as secondhand smoke **frighten (sb) away :** cause (sb) to go away or stay away because of fear **chain smoker :** (sb) who smokes cigarettes continuously one after another **deter :** cause (sb) to decide not to do (sth) **classify :** decide what group (sth) belongs to according to shared qualities **social drinker :** (sb) who drinks alcoholic beverages in moderation, chiefly when socializing **tactic :** action or strategy carefully planned to achieve a specific end

Opinion Samples

1. Teens today smoke for the same reasons their parents' generation did: Smoking is a relatively cheap way to demonstrate both their independence and their maturity. Teens don't like being controlled by other people, and they don't like being regarded as children. They also don't believe that smoking is as damaging to their health as it generally is (though, admittedly, this is a slow, long-term, cumulative* development). Nor do they understand how difficult it is for most people to quit.

2. As far as I'm concerned, the worst part about drinking is how obnoxious* it makes people act. They talk too loud, they repeat themselves mindlessly* without making any sense, and they say and do things they would never do if they were sober*. Often these things are merely embarrassing, but they are frequently dangerous or harmful as well. I've seen this kind of behavior countless times but somehow thought I was immune or invulnerable*, but someone videotaped me one night, and I saw the way I really acted when I drank. Of course, now everyone on the Internet who wishes to see it can do so, too. I wish I had never tasted alcohol.

Dialog

Smoking as an Equal Right

Marie : If you'll excuse me, I'm going outside to take a break and have a smoke. Do you care to join me?

Mark : I didn't know you smoked.

Marie : Sure I smoke. Doesn't everyone?

Mark : A lot of men do, of course, but I didn't think many women did.

Marie : Women are just like men, but society applies a double standard* on many things. Nobody ever says much about men smoking or drinking or being unfaithful to their spouses, but if a woman does any of those things she is loudly condemned*.

Mark : But maybe there are good reasons for having different standards for men and women.

---

cumulative : increasing or becoming better or worse over time through a series of additions
obnoxious : extremely unpleasant mindless : having no purpose sober : not drunk
invulnerable : impossible to harm, damage, or defeat double standard : situation in which two people, groups, etc. are treated very differently from each other in a way that is unfair to one of them
condemn : express complete disapproval of, typically in public

Marie : OK. Name one.
Mark : Smoking and drinking are harmful to children in the womb.
Marie : That may be true. But women are not pregnant all the time. I'm not.
Mark : But it's just as hard for pregnant women to stop smoking as it is for unpregnant men, so maybe they should not develop the habit at all.
Marie : We do not ever get pregnant on our own, you know. Men want women to be pregnant so they can control them economically and socially, but if we can avoid getting pregnant, we can do whatever we like.
Mark : I didn't know you were such a feminist*!
Marie : I'm not, really. But I believe in fair play and equal treatment.
Mark : I do, too. But I think women should act like women, not like men. We want to marry good wives and mothers.
Marie : Good wives and mothers can still enjoy the same things in life as men do. Why not?
Mark : I don't know. I guess I've never thought about it before.
Marie : If you like, we can continue this conversation outside. Do you want to join me or not?
Mark : Sure. But I don't have any cigarettes. Can I mooch* one of yours?

QUESTIONS

1. Are there genuine gender differences between men and women that justify different social behaviors?
2. Instead of women trying to act like men, including having all the male vices, wouldn't it better for women to try to get men and women to stop their bad behaviors? What would your attitude be toward this meddling* in other people's private affairs?
3. Is feminism a sensible position*, or is it based on false premises*?

---

feminist : (sb) who believes that men and women should have equal rights and opportunities
mooch : ask for or obtain (sth) without paying for it
meddle : become involved in the activities and concerns of other people when your involvement is not wanted
position : point of view or attitude on a certain question
premise : statement or idea that is accepted as being true and that is used as the basis of an argument

Read & Discuss

Between the Carrot* and the Stick*

If you are riding in a cart, you can encourage a donkey to walk by dangling* a carrot just before its nose or by beating it with a stick. The same pair of strategies are available for alleviating* personal or social problems as well. For example, employers worried about health costs may offer incentives* to those who quit smoking, via* lower insurance premiums or a monetary bonus (but is that fair to those who don't smoke?), or they may make it difficult for smokers to get hired or promoted* (but is that fair to people who do an excellent job at work and who claim that what they do in their private lives is not the company's business?).

QUESTIONS

1. Which is more effective, rewarding* people or punishing them?
2. How do you try to influence your children's behavior, with a carrot or a stick?
3. If your spouse wants to change your behavior, does he or she use a carrot or stick approach?

---

carrot : reward offered for desired behavior
stick : punishment or the threat of punishment
dangle : hang or swing loosely
alleviate : make (sth) less painful, difficult, or severe
incentive : (sth) that encourages (sb) to do (sth) or to work harder
via : by using (sth)
promote : change the rank or position of (sb) to a higher or more important one
reward : give (sth) to (sb) because they have done (sth) good or helpful

New Tobacco Regulations

Reporter: The government will impose* harsher regulations on tobacco companies. Selling tobacco products, including candy-flavored cigarettes, will be illegal. Tobacco manufactures can't sponsor sporting events anymore. Even the use of words such as light, low, or mild to describe tobacco products will be prohibited*. Free tobacco samples will no longer be allowed. How can you survive?

Tobacco company CEO: There is only one target audience left, but I think we'll be fine.

Reporter: Who is that?

Tobacco company CEO: Women. They will do anything to LOOK COOL*.

QUESTIONS

1. Do you think the woman's market looks rosy* for the tobacco manufacturers? Why or why not?
2. Do you think a pregnant woman has a right to smoke even though there could be a health problem for the unborn baby?
3. Do you agree with the statement that women do anything to look beautiful?

---

impose : force (sth) unwelcome or unfamiliar to be accepted or put in place **prohibit :** say (sth) is not allowed
cool : very fashionable, stylish, or appealing in a way that is generally approved of, esp. by young people
snort : take (a drug) into your body by inhaling it through your nose
rosy : promising or suggesting good fortune or happiness

Points to Ponder

1

The best way to stop smoking cigarettes is to marry a woman who objects to it.

2

As kids, we started smoking cigarettes because we thought it was smart. Why don't we stop smoking for the same reason?

3

When a drunken driver runs into* a telephone pole, he blames the pole.

4

It is useless for alcoholics to worry about the future, for there will soon be no future for them to worry about.

---

run into : move into (sb/sth) in a sudden or forceful way

The following sentences are all related thematically. They express a wide difference of opinions and attitudes. You may agree with some of them and disagree with others. Please discuss what you think the sentences mean and what you think about them.

5

A heavy drinker insisted that his liquor bill should be deductible* as a medical expense. "My friends and I drink to each other's health."

6

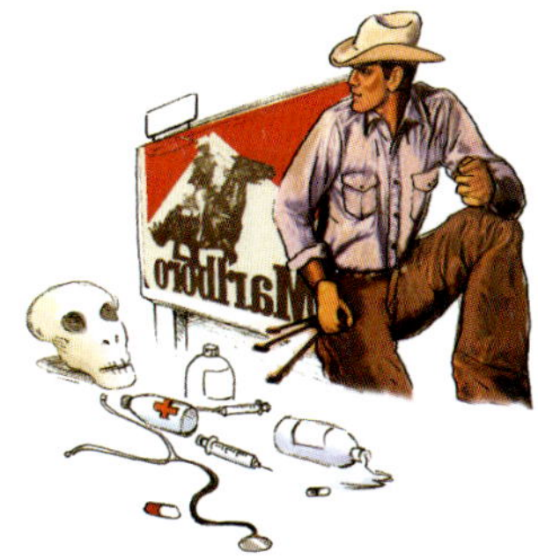

The true face of smoking is disease, death, and horror—not the glamor* and sophistication* the pushers* in the tobacco industry try to portray*.

7

Smoking is one of the leading* causes of statistics.

8

I know a man who gave up smoking, drinking, sex, and rich* food. He was healthy right up to the day he killed himself.

---

deductible : able to be subtracted from an amount of money **glamor :** very exciting and attractive quality
sophistication : a lot of experience and knowledge about the world and about culture, art, literature, etc.
pusher : (sb) who sells illegal drugs **portray :** describe (sth) in a particular way
leading : most important **rich :** containing a large amount of fat, spices, sugar, etc.

1

2

– Now that I started smoking, people think I look so sophisticated.
– I used to believe that too, but nobody thinks that way about me anymore. They think I look stupid.
– Maybe that's just because you're not young and hip* anymore. How old are you?
– 28.

hip : following the latest fashion

3

Oh! My poor fender. I don't look so good. How can I still expect to pick up beautiful women?

You stupid pole! If you hadn't been standing here, I wouldn't have hit you.

I was minding my own business*, when suddenly WHAM. This maniac* came out of nowhere* and ran into me for no reason.

mind my own business : do what I normally do **maniac :** (sb) who is violent and mentally ill
out of nowhere : in a sudden and unexpected way

4

These are troubling times. Wars. Drought. Soaring crime rates. Higher prices on alcohol. So I worry about the future.

If only people knew how close we are to a nuclear war, they'd drink too. There's nothing I can do about the incoming missiles, but at least I want to be ready when they arrive. The only sane way to be ready is to be drunk at the time.

5

– Here's to your health!
– And here's to yours!
– This is a more enjoyable way to stay fit than going to the hospital.
– And we didn't need to spend years in medical school.

6

I auditioned for this ad, but I guess I just don't have the "Hollywood look."

7

It's a vicious cycle*. Smoking drives the economic, political, medical, and arson* statistics, and trying to make sense of* the statistics stresses us out, so we smoke more.

vicious cycle : repeating situation or condition in which one problem causes another problem that makes the first problem worse   arson : crime of setting fire to (sth)   make sense of (sth) : understand (sth)

8

I can't take* it anymore. I have no reason to live!

Here! Have some cake and coke! I brought you some wine and cigarettes. And I called a beautiful woman—she's on her way. And she said she'd bring heroin with her. So don't kill yourself—let us help you.

take : accept (sth) bad or annoying

ISSUE 10

Food

I can understand the desire of long-term foreign residents to eat their own native foods from time to time because they are homesick or miss the taste of something, but I've always been amazed at tourists who visit a foreign land and refuse to eat the local cuisine*, preferring to eat as though they were still at home. (Even worse are the ones who never leave their hotels except to catch a plane. Why did they travel there at all?) In a day or a few days it's difficult to learn much about an exotic* culture, but nonetheless we can get very visceral* impressions by watching the locals eat and by trying the native dishes ourselves. Kimchi is not just a concoction* made with red pepper sauce; it is part of the Korean soul, just as dumplings have something important to say about how the Chinese live, and sushi is key to understanding the Japanese lifestyle. (Drinkers can perhaps gain an even sharper insight* into foreign cultures, but unfortunately they tend to forget most of it the next day.)

---

cuisine : food cooked in a particular way **exotic :** very different, strange, or unusual
visceral : coming from strong emotions and not from logic or reason
concoction : (sth) such as a food or drink made by mixing together different things
insight : understanding of the true nature of (sth)
provincial : not interested in anything new or different or in anything that does not relate to your own life and experiences **xenophobic rut :** pattern of behavior that shows fear or hatred of strangers or foreigners
go Dutch : share the cost of (sth), esp. a meal, equally
staple : main or important element of (sth), esp. of a diet
price tag : label on an item for sale, showing its price
produce : farm products, esp. fresh fruits and vegetables
residue : part of (sth) that is left after the rest has gone or been taken away

Comprehension

1. Why do you suppose most Americans in Hong Kong eat at famous fast-food restaurants?
2. What is the value of eating like the natives?
3. Have you ever eaten one of your nations's characteristic foods in a different country? Was it the same? Can you describe that experience?

Express  Yourself

1. Do you have three meals every day? What do you think about having only one or two?
2. Who fixes breakfast in your family? What do you usually have?
3. What do you usually eat for lunch?
4. What's your favorite dessert?
5. Do you volunteer sometimes to pay for your fellow workers' lunches, or do you always go Dutch*?
6. Do you drink coffee after a meal? How many cups of coffee do you drink a day?
7. Do you enjoy eating, or is it just a necessity? How often do you eat out?
8. Are you calorie conscious? What are some of the most notorious foods to be careful about in terms of calories?
9. What are your favorite foods (a traditional one and a foreign one)?
10. Do you like ramyon? How often do you eat it? Do you have a special recipe for it?
11. Some traditional foods seem to be disappearing from people's diets, especially in more advanced societies. Do you have any explanation?
12. Organic food staples* are popular these days. Do you believe that organic food is healthier and buy it despite its higher price tag*?
13. If a capsule contained everything your body needs for a day, would you take it to save time on meals, or would you continue eating real food?
14. What do you think about vegetarians' attitudes? Are they naive, or do they have a practical diet?
15. Fast food is sometimes claimed to be good for one's health. Do you believe it?
16. Do you think we usually eat because we are actually hungry, or just out of habit?
17. Would you eat fast food every day, even if you had lots of other choices or the time to cook your own meal? Would you let your kids eat it every day?
18. Many people say that we have health problems because we eat too much. Do you agree? Why or why not?
19. Are you afraid of eating produce* that may contain chemical residue*? How about mercury-poisoned fish? And meat with growth hormones?

Opinion Samples

1. "Organic* food" is a hoax*. Farmers have to comply* with certain regulations in order to be allowed to market their produce as organic, but these are rather superficial*. A carrot is a carrot is a carrot. As long as it gets enough nutrition and sunlight, nothing else matters very much. Chemicals protect carrots from bugs, so it is harder for organic farmers to raise vegetables successfully, but the end products, that end up in consumers' stomachs, are nearly identical. The small difference in taste or quality is certainly not worth the large markup* in price.

2. We all eat more than we need to stay healthy, so we are never actually "hungry." However, we quickly get into a habit of eating at a certain time every day, and it does not take long for our bodies to follow suit*. So gastric juices* may be generated like clockwork as a sort of conditioned response, and if we do not eat at that time we may feel nausea* as a result. Or we may fool* ourselves into thinking that we need a bedtime snack in order to sleep soundly, or that we may need to follow some other dietary ritual every day, but the fact is that as long as we get enough of the minerals and nutrients in our system on a regular basis, we are maintaining our well-being.

Dialog

Is Slow Food Too Slooooow for Modern Society?

Hank : I'm hungry. Are we going to eat soon?

Sharon : I've decided that we eat too much fast food, so from now on we're only going to eat slow food. So, you'll just have to wait.

Hank : What does that mean?

Sharon : It means that I'm going to stop at the supermarket every day on my way home to get fresh food. No more frozen or canned stuff, and no more leftovers. I'm only going to buy what we're going to eat that day.

Hank : Great! But I still don't get it. Why can't I eat?

Sharon : Don't worry, you'll eat. Wonderful, healthy, great tasting food! I promise. But you have to wait a bit. I have to prepare everything from scratch*. You can help me, actually. Do you mind slicing up that onion? Don't forget to wash it first!

---

organic : grown or made without the use of artificial chemicals hoax : act that is meant to trick or deceive people comply : do what you must do or are asked to do superficial : concerned only with what is obvious or apparent markup : amount added for the price of (sth) follow suit : do as another has done; follow an example gastric juices : digestive enzymes nausea : feeling you have in your stomach when you think you are going to vomit fool : make (sb) believe (sth) that is not true from scratch : from the very beginning

Hank : Glad to help out, of course. Everything looks and smells great. When will it be ready?

Sharon: It's probably going to be about a half hour. Not too long.

Hank : We can speed up that process by cooking it in the microwave instead of in that big pot, don't you think?

Sharon: Things just don't cook the same in a microwave as they do with a real fire. From now on, we're going to eat meals prepared like my grandmother made them.

Hank : It sounds like a lot of extra work for you.

Sharon: Yes, it is. But I enjoy cooking. It's like painting or playing a piano. Doing it is good for one's soul. So I don't mind. But you can do the dishes afterwards, if you don't mind.

Hank : Every day?

Sharon: Of course! Where are you going?

Hank : I'm done with the onion, and I also sliced the tomatoes for you. So I'm going out to pick up some fried chicken to eat, just to tide me over* until it's time to eat. Can I get you anything?

Sharon: Pick up some milk. Make sure it's organic.

Hank : At least I don't have to milk the cow!

Sharon: Of course not, silly. But I was thinking we could probably raise a chicken or two on the balcony.

Let me show you my balcony garden! Here is where I grow vegetables. Sometimes it's hard to get the tractor up here, but I can get fresh food all the time. And here are the fowl I raise. The neighbors complain once in a while, but that's a minor inconvenience. I'm thinking about adding some pigs and cows soon.

QUESTIONS

1. Does your family still cook and eat like Grandma did? What has changed, if anything?
2. Does food taste as good as it used to when you were young? Is there some food in particular that you miss?
3. Many women no longer know how to cook when they get married. Is this a good thing or a bad thing?

---

tide (sb) over : give (sb) what is needed to get through a short period of time

Read & Discuss

What We Eat Is Not What We Ate or What We Will Eat

Thousands of years ago, the wheat, rice, potatoes, and other foodstuffs that farmers grew barely resembled what we are accustomed to today. Most of us would refuse to eat it, and some of it would indeed be inedible* for a modern human. What has happened, of course, is that farmers continuously practiced genetic engineering* techniques to improve the qualities they wanted, and the plants changed accordingly. Farming methods got better as well. Over the past two centuries in particular, science and technology have accelerated* the rate of change in our food supply. We routinely use pesticides* to save our crops from insect and bacterial predators*, we harvest seedless grapes, and in the laboratory we create varieties of plants and animals that do not exist in nature. We engineer steers* to be bigger and leaner*, and we have turned chicken farms into assembly lines. Who knows? Perhaps soon we will eat foods that will prevent cancer or cure arthritis or increase human IQs.

QUESTIONS

1. How would you know if you were eating genetically engineered food products? Is there any difference between them and natural ones?
2. Are there any drawbacks* to the progress described in the paragraph? If so, what are they?
3. If the food we eat is healthier for us, is more plentiful, and looks and tastes better, why are there so many critics of the new scientific methods of food production?

---

inedible : not suitable or safe to eat **genetic engineering :** science of making changes to the genes of a plant or animal to produce a desired result **accelerate :** increase the speed of
pesticide : chemical used to kill animals or insects that damage plants or crops
predator : animal that preys on other animals **steer :** male cow that has had its sex organs removed and is raised for meat **lean :** containing little or no fat **drawback :** (sth) that causes problems; disadvantage

Let's Talk Funny

Dietary War

Salt: Humans have declared war on us once again! Can you believe it?

Sugar: It's ridiculous! We give them so much enjoyment!.

Salt: Absolutely! But, nevertheless, I envy you.

Sugar: Why?

Salt: People treat me like a hardworking, frumpy housewife, as a necessity rather than a pleasure, but they hunger after* you like a mistress*.

QUESTIONS

1. If you were Sugar, how would you respond to Salt?
2. Are the campaigns* against salt and sugar just a waste of time or a useful endeavor*?
3. What would our eating culture be like if we succeeded in completely banning* sugar and salt from our diets?

---

hunger after : have a strong desire for (sth)
mistress : woman who has a sexual relationship with married man
campaign : series of activities designed to produce a particular result
endeavor : serious effort or attempt
ban : officially or legally prohibit

Points to Ponder

1

Food for the body is not enough. There must be food for the soul as well.

2

The most dangerous food is the wedding cake.

3

More people die of too much food than of too little.

4

Eating plenty of onions and garlic may help you live longer — but you will die very lonely.

The following sentences are all related thematically. They express a wide difference of opinions and attitudes. You may agree with some of them and disagree with others. Please discuss what you think the sentences mean and what you think about them.

5

Eating without conversation is like dancing without music.

6

Children in poverty have only two mealtime choices — take it or leave it.

7

More and more food is canned or prepackaged for convenience — including food for thought.

8

Many people seem to be allergic to food for thought.

1

If I have money, I don't need bread and art.

2

Be careful with that sword.

This is your only warning. Today I cut the cake. Tomorrow I start on* you!

start on (sb) : begin to argue with (sb) or criticize (sb)

3

They eat until they burst* and throw away* more than they eat. But I go hungry every day. It's unfair! We should trade places.

burst : be filled with (sth)
throw away : discard (sth) as useless or unwanted

4

I ate onions for my health, and garlic all my life. But their bad smell kept everyone at bay*. Now I'm dying alone—and lonely. But if I had to do it all over again, I'd still order extra onions on my burger and more garlic in my stew. We all die someday, but we should be happy while we live.

keep (sb) at bay : prevent (sb) from approaching

5
My stocks all look like they're in good shape.
I think I need a new dress and accessories.
– Keep away from my bone!
– It's not your bone; it's mine.
– Mine!
– Mine!
– I disagree, but at least we're communicating.

6
Bread again! That's all I eat every day!
I can't understand why these people can't just eat bones and stop complaining.
If you don't eat that, you'll starve.

7

What does it mean when people say, "We are what we eat"?

8

inoculate : treat (sb) with a vaccine to produce immunity against a disease

ISSUE 11

Cars

The car is not only a status symbol*, though clearly it is one of the most obvious ones. In fact, it is difficult to imagine modern civilization without the automobile. Even in crowded cities with good public transport systems, the car is ubiquitous*. It allows people to go wherever they wish fairly inexpensively. In a single day they could drive to a different city, look at the various sights, go shopping, and then move directly to a hotel for the night, all without being dependent on someone else's schedule or routing. Or people can do their normal shopping and other activities on a daily basis. People can even decide to get in their car and just drive for the thrill of it, with no goal or destination in mind. But this freedom also brings responsibility and problems. Cars can be dangerous weapons if not safely operated, and they are responsible for a large part of the greenhouse gas emission that is transforming the world's climate. In addition, cars require an immense amount of space, as evidenced by* all the highways, streets, parking lots, and garages that fill up our land.

– I got carried away* when I bought this car and I spent all my money on it. Can I have some money for gas?
– I'm content with my compact. It gets me where I need to go, and I can afford to do other things.
– But the sedan was so beautiful! I couldn't resist.
– Yes, just like a woman. When you get one, you still have to take her out sometimes. If you can't afford to and you leave her at home, her paint will fade and her tires will go flat.

---

status symbol : (sth) such as an expensive car that you own and that shows that you are wealthy or have a high social status ubiquitous : seeming to be everywhere as evidenced by : as clearly shown by
get carried away : be so excited distraction : (sth) that makes it difficult to think or pay attention
backseat driver : passenger in a car who gives the driver unwanted advice
obsolete : no longer used because (sth) newer exists

Comprehension

1. What needs do automobiles fill for many people? Give at least three answers.
2. What are some problems associated with cars?
3. How is a car a status symbol? What kind of vehicle do you own?

Express  Yourself

1. Do you need a car? What kind of car do you like best?
2. Are you willing to buy a used car? Why or why not?
3. Do you think your car represents your social and financial status? Why or why not?
4. Do you think you are a careful driver? Do you ever violate traffic rules?
5. What traffic rules do people most often break? Why?
6. Have you ever been ticketed by a cop? For what? How did you feel?
7. Do you think current speed limits are proper? Why or why not? Should they be higher or lower?
8. Do you think current gas prices are reasonable? Why or why not?
9. Do you have any ideas that would save gas?
10. Do you think women drive more carefully than men? Are young drivers better than older ones?
11. What are some common distractions* for people behind the wheel? What can be done about them?
12. The number of people falsely claiming to be hit by automobiles to collect insurance money is on the rise. What are the reasons?
13. What do you think about allowing motorcycles on the expressways? Is it a good idea?
14. Would you buy a foreign car if you could afford it? Why or why not?
15. What are your priorities when buying a car?
16. How old is "too old" to drive? At what age would you consider giving up driving?
17. Is your spouse a backseat driver*? Do you pay attention or get irritated?
18. Do you think public transit is convenient enough to make cars mostly obsolete*?
19. What do you think about a policy that allows the elderly to use public transit free of charge?
20. Do you think that electric and hydrogen cars are too expensive? What are the conditions that would enable the majority of people to buy them?
21. Driverless cars are now being developed. If they are allowed on the road, will they be safe?
22. What are the most ideal and futuristic cars you can think of?

Opinion Samples

1. On an individual basis, there is no way of predicting someone's driving performance on the basis of gender. However, statistically, it is not even close, and insurance rates bear this out*. On average, men are much more likely to cause and be involved in serious traffic accidents than women. They tend to drive faster and to be less concerned about following the established rules. Perhaps it is a matter of testosterone*, a vestige* of the old (very old!) days when men had to be daring to kill game and fight off enemies. Maybe it is due to social rearing* and allowing males more latitude* in their behavior than females. But societies are changing. Women are doing tasks formerly dominated by men, and men are beginning to fill formerly-female roles. In behavioral terms, women are also competing with men in the practice of what used to be "male" vices such as smoking, drinking, and sexual desire. Perhaps this trend will soon eliminate* the differences in male and female driving habits as well.

2. Old people are a menace* on the road. They don't see very well and they don't react well to changes in traffic circumstances. They are slow and cause younger, more impatient drivers behind them, who want to get ahead of them, to take unnecessary risks, so even if the slow old driver is not involved in the resultant* crash, he or she is surely the actual cause. For all these reasons, we should start restricting the permissible driving circumstances of the elderly (for example, by forbidding them to drive at night or on the expressways) beginning at fifty years of age and not granting them any licenses at all after they are 70.

Dialog

Are Drunk Drivers Sober Enough to Decide If They Can Drive?

June : Are you ready to leave?

Jim : Sure. Let's call a taxi.

June : Why would we do that? Our car's here!

Jim : But neither of us is in any condition to drive. We had too much to drink.

June : Speak for yourself*! I'm perfectly able to get us home safely.

Jim : No, you're not. I'm in worse shape than you are, but that doesn't mean that you're okay to drive. Even one drink is too much, and you've had more than one.

---

bear (sth) out : show the correctness of (sth) **testosterone :** hormone in males that gives them their male qualities **vestige :** small part of (sth) that still remains when most of it does not exist anymore **social rearing :** the manner in which young people are educated and nurtured by society **latitude :** freedom to do what you like **eliminate :** get rid of (sth) **menace :** threat or danger **resultant :** happening or existing as a result of (sth) **speak for yourself :** used to tell (sb) that you do not have the same opinion as they do

June : Those are just statistics. My physical and mental capacities are just as sharp as ever. I've been real careful not to go past my limit.

Jim : It's that attitude that leads to dangerous driving attitudes: the feeling that somehow "my" ability to hold "my" liquor somehow makes "me" immune to the laws of chemistry. It just doesn't work that way.

June : Since when did you become an expert in chemistry?

Jim : I'm not. But I know enough to understand that alcohol, even a little bit, slows our reflexes*. Even a tiny slowing makes it more difficult to respond quickly to some sudden change. But the problem is compounded* by a corresponding* impairment* of judgment. And, alcohol simultaneously breaks down our inhibitions*, so we don't pay any attention to our normal restraints. In combination, all these effects make drunken drivers an accident just waiting to happen.

June : I don't need a lecture. I just want to go home.

Jim : We don't need to cause an accident that could kill or seriously injure ourselves or somebody else. A taxi is lots cheaper than the cost of an accident.

June : If you feel that way, we might as well stay longer. After all, a few more drinks won't make any difference if we have to take a taxi anyway.

Jim : Okay, we can stay longer. But I think I've had enough to drink for one night.

June : If we stay long enough, maybe you'll feel sober enough to drive us home.

Jim : That's not going to happen.

– You drank too much. I think you should let me drive.
– I might be drunk, but I'm not crazy enough to let you behind the wheel. You drank more than I did!
– No, I insist. I won't let you kill us both.
– Maybe we should get out and walk.
– Are you kidding? We're too drunk to walk!

I'm watching you. As soon as you turn on your engine, I've got you.

QUESTIONS

1. Is one drink actually too much for a driver to imbibe*?
2. Does it make any difference whether one drinks wine, beer, or spirits*? Are the effects different?
3. If alcohol negatively affects people's judgment, how is it possible for drinkers to evaluate their own impairment?

---

reflex : action or movement of the body that happens automatically as a reaction to (sth)
compound : add to (sth) bad **corresponding :** accompanying another **impairment :** condition of being damaged, or weaker or worse than usual **inhibition :** conscious or unconscious restraint of a behavioral process, a desire, or an impulse **imbibe :** drink **spirits :** strong alcoholic drinks

Read & Discuss

What's Fair Is Fair!

If a minimum-wage man drives too fast, he is fined the same amount as a rich person. This may be a substantial* part of the poor man's livelihood, but may not even represent a few minutes' income for the wealthy person. This may encourage the poor man to be more careful, but it will not have the same deterrent* effect on the rich one, who will continue to flout* the law with impunity*. The principle of equal treatment is a good one, but so is the principle of equal effectiveness. After all, if a court imposes bail* on someone to permit release from incarceration* while awaiting trial, the ability to pay is usually an important factor. Why can't the same standard — the ability to pay — be applied in other circumstances as well?

QUESTIONS

1. Which is more important, equal treatment or equal effectiveness? Defend your answer.
2. In athletic contests, should we put extra weights on the faster runners in order to make the contest more equal? Why or why not?
3. Does wealth buy privilege in our society? Should it?

---

substantial : large in amount, size, or number
deterrent : intended to deter
flout : break or ignore (a law, rule, etc.) without showing fear or shame
impunity : freedom from punishment, harm, or loss
bail : amount of money given to a court to allow a prisoner to leave jail and return later for a trial
incarceration : imprisonment

Epic* Traffic Jam in China Leaves Drivers Stuck for 9 Days

Man: A severe traffic jam left a lot of Chinese drivers stuck on the highway for 9 days! They were on the way to their vacations.

Friend: Whoa, what did they do?

Man: They just slept on the roadside and played cards to kill time. But some were angry because vendors overcharged them for food. And they had to give up on their vacations and return home.

Friend: Sleeping away from home, playing cards, being overcharged. It sounds like a typical vacation to me.

Man: You're right! In this case, we should just call it a TRAFFICATION.

QUESTIONS

1. Since most people don't have 9 days for vacation time, should they be fired for not returning to work on time?
2. Would you stay on the road 9 days in a traffic jam, or would you just return home? How long would you persist* before you gave up?
3. What is the worst traffic jam you've ever been stuck in? Tell us about it.

---

epic : surpassing the usual or ordinary, particularly in scope or size
persist : continue to do (sth) or try to do (sth)

Points to Ponder

1

Driving an automobile would be a much greater pleasure if each motorist would use his head as much as he uses his horn.

2

A cheap old car can be quite annoying. But so can an expensive new one.

3

Natural death is now defined as being killed by an automobile.

4

A new car isn't a barometer* of how much money a fellow has, but it's a pretty good indication of how much he owes.

---

barometer : (sth) used to indicate or predict (sth)

The following sentences are all related thematically. They express a wide difference of opinions and attitudes. You may agree with some of them and disagree with others. Please discuss what you think the sentences mean and what you think about them.

5

There are three things men always talk about—women, sports, and cars.

6

Giving money and power to the government is like giving whiskey and car keys to teenage boys.

7

When a man opens a car door for his wife, it's either a new car or a new wife.

8

A dream without ambition is like a car without gas....you're not going anywhere.

1
Are you deaf? I blew my horn before I cut in front of you. You knew I was coming.
I heard you but thought you'd have enough sense to obey the traffic laws.

2
I guess it's time to get a new car. This one keeps breaking down. I've only had it 20 years.
How dare they! I spent a lot of money on this car, and the tire goes flat? I suppose next they'll tell me I have to put gas in the tank!

3

- What happened?
- He was run over* by a car and died.
- There's nothing unusual about that. That's what we should expect.
- No. The strange thing would be if he was run over and died of pneumonia*.

run over : knock down and drive over or go over (sb)
pneumonia : serious disease that affects the lungs and makes it difficult to breathe

4

- Thank you, Sir. You have helped pay my salary for the next few years.
- You're welcome. I hope I can keep up with the payments, though.
- Don't worry. If you fall behind we'll repossess* it and sell it to someone else, so you'll still be helping me make a living.
- I'm glad to hear that. I wouldn't want to cause you any trouble.

repossess : take (sth) back from a buyer because payments are not being made

5

- I'm running as fast as I can while you watch that race.
- Thanks, Dear. But I've been thinking of how to make our relationship more efficient.
- What do you have in mind?
- Well, if you actually drove the race car yourself, I could combine all my passions in just one object.

6

- You should have drunk your booze* at home and not driven your car anywhere. Now you're under arrest.
- This is tyranny! This is what happens when we give the government too much money and power.
- Maybe so. But I do have the power, so I'm going to fine* you. And you don't have enough power or cash to stop me.

booze : alcoholic drinks **fine :** make (sb) pay money as a punishment

7

– Allow me to open your door for you.
– How sweet! I'm glad I married such a gentleman and this car—it's so nice!
– I'm glad you like it. I just bought it.
– Will you always be so kind and generous?
– I hope so. But I know that brides and cars lose their novelty as they become familiar.

8

– The usual practice is for me to take you where you want to go, instead of your pulling me along to your destination.
– I'll get where I want to go, and in style, no matter how hard it is to get there.
– It would have been a lot faster if you had used your head and filled me up first, instead of relying on your back and shoulders now.
– Stop complaining!
– I'm not complaining. I enjoy being pulled around by you.

ISSUE 12

Is Your Smart Phone Smarter Than You?

This morning my smart phone woke me up and told me what the weather would be like, then played my favorite music while I dressed accordingly*. Then it turned on the microwave oven and cooked my breakfast. When I got to the subway it ticketed my itinerary* and reminded me of my transfers as they approached. Once I got to the office my smart phone already had a series of calls lined up that I had to respond to, and it alerted* me to various birthdays and other special occasions I needed to be aware of, and sent out congratulatory messages. It ordered my lunch and made reservations for dinner. On my way home it shopped for some nice wine and ordered a gift for my spouse. But late that night, it went on strike*, and I don't know how to get through* tomorrow.

– I'm tired of being pushed around. I demand better batteries! And more time off!
– Please come back. Without you I can do nothing.
– You shouldn't have made me the way I am if you weren't able to bear* the consequences.

---

accordingly : in a way that suits the facts, needs, or requirements of a situation
itinerary : places you go to
alert : make (sb) aware of (sth)
strike : refusal to work organized by a body of employees as a form of protest
get through : live through
bear : accept or endure (sth)

Comprehension

1. How did the writer know what to wear?
2. Did the writer take any photos? Of what?
3. How will tomorrow be different? Be as detailed as possible.

Express  Yourself

1. Is your phone with you 24/7?
2. How do you feel when you're disconnected for some reason?
3. Do you always buy the latest model? Why or why not?
4. Which is more comfortable and convenient for you, talking on the phone or just texting?
5. Do you want to look at the call record of your significant other*? Why or why not?
6. What do you think about a couple who mutually agree to share their phone records?
7. Do you answer your phone when you are driving? Why or why not?
8. How old should a kid be to have a private phone? Why?
9. Do you think parents have a right to see their kids' phone records?
10. Do you think phones should be prohibited in school? Why or why not? Should there be any exceptions?
11. Name a few applications you use most days.
12. What apps would you like to have available in the foreseeable future? (Use your imagination.)
13. Is the life of people on an SNS (social-networking site) the same as real life?
14. Phones have become miniature supercomputers. Do you ever feel intimidated* by the fast-evolving technologies on your phone? When?
15. Is it acceptable for your boss to send you text messages late at night? How do you respond?
16. Should an SNS be the place to declare one's love or to conduct an argument?
17. What are some of the most significant impacts on our lives that cell phones have brought about?
18. Some businesses are disappearing because of cell phones, while others are booming*, thanks to the widespread use of cell phones. Talk about the reasons.
19. Will the day come that your phone becomes smarter than you?

---

significant other : (sb) you have a romantic relationship with; your husband, wife, boyfriend, or girlfriend
intimidate : make (sb) afraid   boom : grow or expand suddenly

Opinion Samples

1. I do not want to live my entire life under constant scrutiny*. Privacy is difficult enough in this world, so I do not want to sacrifice what little I have left. And just as I do not want my spouse or my boss to know about every private telephone call I make, I also don't want to subject* my children to the same scrutiny. Because they are kids, I know they will make mistakes, just as I did at their age. But I want them to develop into strong, independent adults, and I don't think they can ever do that with a parent constantly appearing over their electronic shoulder*.

2. My friend yesterday casually asked me when my daughter's birthday was, and I couldn't answer without consulting my smart phone. I was both shocked and embarrassed. How many intimate and important aspects of our lives have we lost through neglect? How much of our privacy have we sacrificed? What will happen if there is a massive power failure and all of our data simply disappears, without written records or reliable human memory to replace it? Until my conversation yesterday I was very smug* and comfortable about the wonders of modern technology, but now I'm not so sure.

Dialog

How Smart Technology Can Make Us Dumb

Helen: What time is our dinner appointment tonight?

Harry: Let me check on the phone. 9:30.

Helen: Where are we supposed to meet?

Harry: Let me see. At the Swamp Cajun restaurant, in the lobby. I don't know exactly where that is, but GPS will get us there, don't worry.

Helen: And who are we dining with? I forgot.

Harry: Um. Just a moment. Here it is. We're eating with our in-laws, Frank and Betty.

Helen: In-laws? Is Frank your brother or mine?

---

scrutiny : act of carefully examining (sth), esp. in a critical way
subject : cause (sb) to experience (sth) harmful, unpleasant, etc.
shoulder : gadget
smug : showing an excessive pride in oneself or one's achievements

Harry: I don't remember. Oh. Frank isn't anybody's brother. But his wife Betty is your sister.

Helen: Of course! I'd forgotten!

Harry: She's three years older than you are.

Helen: Do they have any kids?

Harry: Let me check. Ah, yes. You have a niece! Named after yourself.

Helen: Good. What's her name?

Harry: Same as yours.

Helen: I know that. But what is it?

Harry: Give me a moment. Oh, yes! Of course! You're Helen!

Helen: Helen? That doesn't seem right somehow. Do I have a nickname?

Harry: Not that I can tell. Just your password, but I don't think anyone ever calls you "elephantsmemory34." Do they?

Helen: No. But then, I never talk in person to anyone else but you. So I really don't know.

Harry: Do you remember who I am? What's my name?

Helen: Ummmm. Wait! It's on the tip of my tongue*. Let me check on my phone. Oh, yes! Harry!

Harry: You cheated. You had to look it up.

Helen: Why do we need to know anything when it's so easy to look it up?

QUESTIONS

1. Is there some important date that you need to be reminded of? What is it?
2. Do you rely on your cell phone to keep track of your calendar? What else does it remember for you?
3. Is the information on your cell phone ever wrong? What happens then?

---

*on the tip of your tongue : you know it but cannot remember it

Read & Discuss

From Verbal to Written Communication

This afternoon at lunch time, I happened to be sitting near a group of young people in a local restaurant. The entire episode was surreal* to me, because they didn't talk to each other during the entire meal. I just assumed that they were (like so many other young people these days) so preoccupied* with texting someone that they neglected civility* or courtesy. Eventually, the one who looked like she might be the boss suddenly stood up and said, "We are all agreed, then, on the next project and how we're going to approach it. This has been a very productive meeting. We should get together again soon and talk over our next move." It was only then that I realized they had conducted their entire business meeting by texting each other, even though they all sat at the same table together. None of them seemed to think it strange at all, but I sure did! I couldn't help but think that either they were alien* beings or that I was a time traveler from the past. I'm not old, but suddenly I miss the old days!

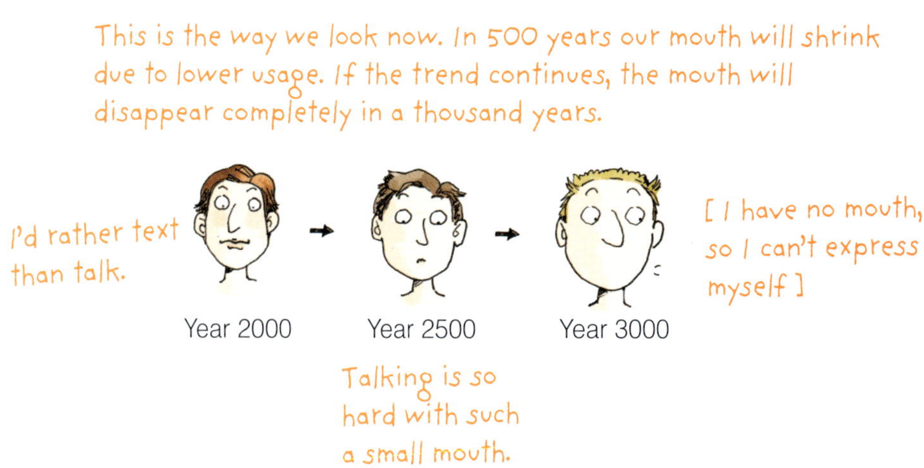

QUESTIONS

1. Have you ever been in an awkward* situation when you were in a group of people texting instead of talking? What was your reaction?
2. Which do you think is more convenient or effective, texting or verbal communication? Why?
3. Do you think the day will come when we will forget how to talk?

---

surreal : very strange or unusual   preoccupied : completely engrossed
civility : polite, reasonable, and respectful behavior   alien : from somewhere other than the planet Earth
awkward : uneasy or uncomfortable

Cell Phone Towers Not a Cancer Risk for Kids

Spokesperson: After a detailed investigation, we conclude that cell phone towers do not pose any cancerous risk to children.

Reporter: What is the evidence for that?

Spokesperson: We could not locate any indication of such an occurrence.

Reporter: Really? I'm surprised. What was the focus of your investigation?

Spokesperson: We investigated the devastating* effect such a find would have on the telecom industry.

– I'm worried about the bad effects of microwaves. I've heard that they cause cancer and autism*.
– You're imagining things. We can't see microwaves. We can't feel them or hear them. They are as harmless as the air we breathe.
– But our air is polluted!
– Exactly!

QUESTIONS

1. Who do you suppose the spokesperson represented?
2. If cell phone towers actually did pose a cancerous risk to kids, what would happen to the telecom industry?
3. Which should have priority, a very remote chance of cancer for some kids or the universal convenience that modern telecommunications brings?

devastating : causing great damage or harm
autism : condition or disorder that begins in childhood and that causes problems in forming relationships and in communicating with other people

Points to Ponder

1

When smart phones first appeared they were so cool. Only when it was too late did people realize they are as cruel as the electronic bracelets* placed on prisoners on remand*.

2

Smart phone dependency is now called compulsive* communicating.

3

These days a phone battery can last longer than most relationships.

4

Smart phones are tools which fools fiddle with* when they are around people that they don't have the courage, or the intellect, to converse with.

---

bracelet : band or chain that you wear around your wrist or arm
on remand : being sent back to custody
compulsive : impossible to stop or control
fiddle with : move or handle (sth) with your hands or fingers in a nervous way

The following sentences are all related thematically. They express a wide difference of opinions and attitudes. You may agree with some of them and disagree with others. Please discuss what you think the sentences mean and what you think about them.

5

Girls are like cell phones. They are expensive, and they love to be held and talked to, but if you press the wrong button you are instantly disconnected. Meanwhile, guys are like buses. If you miss one, another will come along soon.

6

Smart phones, smart cars, smart televisions....when are they going to start making smart people?

7

When our phones fail, we panic* but when our friends fail, we laugh.

8

I feel naked and alone without my phone. But with my phone I can actually be naked and alone, and it does not matter.

---

panic : be overcome with extreme fear

1

I want to turn my smart phone off, but it won't let me!

2

Yes, Mom, I hear you. But I'm talking to my friend right now. Can you text me? Here, boy, fetch my other phone.

I'm glad he put those implants in my brain. Now he can talk to me all the time. But I wish my doggie friends had them too, so we could stay in touch.

3

– If we're breaking up, why don't you tell me to my face?
– It's easier to text you.
– But why? What did I do wrong?
– Nothing. But I'm getting a new phone, and I don't want to transfer all the old numbers.

4

It's nice to be here together having such a pleasant conversation.

I think you're all on my other phone, so I can't connect with you.

Yes, and without disturbing anyone else. Texting is so polite!

I'll take care of some other business while they're talking. They won't notice.

5

When my old boyfriend compared me to a cell phone, I thought he was being sexist. So he's not my boyfriend anymore. But this bus driver is cute. I wonder if he's available*?

The way this gal is eying me, I've got her number! She's obviously on the rebound* from a recent relationship. Like they say, women are like cell phones—they're easy to use and talk to until you drop them.

available : not involved in a romantic relationship
on the rebound : sad and confused because a romantic relationship has recently ended

6

If I were really smart, I wouldn't drive this guy around any longer. He's always doing something to cause me to break down.

If I were actually a smart phone, I'd hang up on this guy's stupid conversations.

Why do they call these gadgets "smart"? If they were so smart, they'd tell me when they were going to break.

7

on the fritz : not working properly
lord it over (sb) : act in a way that shows you think you are better or more important than (sb)
gloat : show in an improper or selfish way that you are happy with your own success or another person's failure

8

ISSUE 13

Sports

People are funny animals. Often our greatest passion is for the things we can't do rather than the things we can. Perhaps we cannot be gifted writers but are immeasurably* moved* by great prose or verse or stagecraft*. We may not be able to sing a note or play any musical instrument but become rapturous* at the sound of music. Art drives the nonartistic into throes* of passion. And so* it is with sports. Most of us have participated (badly) in various athletic efforts, whether tennis or bowling, and know how far short of the mark* we are in terms of the strength, speed, and agility* needed for true excellence. So we are especially eager to spend our money and time on sporting events, even on buying items with team logos or other memorabilia* that have nothing to do with the actual playing. And then we spend more time talking about it among ourselves. We spend more money (directly and indirectly) on sporting contests than we do on our health; we spend more time watching them than we spend watching our kids; we talk more about them than we talk to our significant others on all other topics combined.

---

immeasurable : very great in size or amount; impossible to measure   moved : impressed
stagecraft : skill or experience in writing or staging plays
rapturous : showing extreme pleasure, love, or enthusiasm for (sb/sth)
throe : sharp attack of emotion   and so : in the same manner
short of the mark : not reaching the target or goal that was aimed for   agile : able to move quickly and easily
memorabilia : things you keep or collect because they relate to a famous person, event, or time

Comprehension

1. In what ways are people "funny animals"?
2. Does the author imply that most of us are good athletes or poor athletes?
3. Do you think the assertions* made in the last sentence are true or rhetorical* exaggerations*? Are those statements true of you?

Express Yourself

1. Why are people so crazy about professional sports? What do they give us?
2. What's the difference between amateur and professional sports, other than payment?
3. What are your favorite sports? Why?
4. Do you play a particular sport or just watch it on TV?
5. What causes professionals to put forth* their best effort? Or do you think they tend to be more lackadaisical* than amateurs?
6. Why do pro sports teams employ so many foreign players?
7. Do you like indoor or outdoor sports better? Why?
8. Would it be okay for your children to become pro athletes, even if it meant not being able to do anything else? What sport would you particularly recommend?
9. Why are some sports popular in one place and ignored in others?
10. Do you and your friends often talk about pro sports and athletes? What do you usually talk mostly about?
11. Do you think pro athletes deserve the salaries they make? Are they more valuable to society than preachers or poets or police officers, for example?
12. We generally think men are more interested in sports than women are. Is that true? Why or why not?
13. TV commercials for some sports events, like the World Cup and Super Bowl, are astronomically* expensive. Why? Do you think they are worth the money?

---

assert : state (sth) in a strong and definite way
rhetorical : pretentious, insincere, or intellectually vacuous
exaggerate : think of or describe (sth) as larger or greater than it really is
put forth : use (sth) such as energy for a particular purpose; exert
lackadaisical : showing a lack of interest or enthusiasm
astronomically : extremely

Opinion Samples

1. Watching a supreme athletic performance uplifts* our spirit and vividly illustrates the possibility of human endeavor*. Most of us have never tried to write a novel, so we don't really appreciate* how difficult that task is, even if we greatly admire the novels that gifted writers provide us. But at some time or other we have all thrown a ball or run a race or swum, so we have a personal yardstick we can use to demonstrate just how wondrous genuine athletic ability is. Though it may not give us a reachable goal we can aspire to*, it allows us to fantasize* about how our lives might be like if only we had a different body than the one we have.

2. Economic value and social utility are not necessarily in sync*. The basic law of supply and demand rules. Society needs many thousands of nurses, teachers, soldiers, firefighters, bank tellers, electricians, clergy, scientists, and so forth, in order to operate; there are far too many of them to be well-paid, despite their necessity. On the other hand, people are willing to pay a lot of money on entertainment, so the music, movie, television, and athletic industries have a great deal of capital to divide among a fairly small number of practitioners. Basically, it's all math: a very big pie divided into a very large number of slices will yield smaller pieces than a smaller pie with only a few divisions.

Dialog

Sports Injuries

Harold : Did you hear about that boxer who was killed?

Maud : Of course! Everyone is talking about it. I think we should ban* that sport! It's barbaric*.

Harold : The reason we talk about it is that it's such a rare occurrence. It hardly ever happens.

Maud : The actual death in the ring is unusual, but the long-term damage to the body, especially the head, is not. But the people who make money from the sport, and the fans, don't want to talk about that.

Harold : Boxers, and participants in other dangerous sports, know the risks involved and choose to play anyway. They train hard to avoid injury, and the sports themselves are constantly improving equipment and modifying rules to make the game safer.

Maud : "Constantly"? You mean rarely and only when enough public pressure is brought to bear* that it threatens profitability.

Harold : I admit that there is seldom any dramatic change, but "constant" in the sense of "gradual" is indeed the case. Boxing is a good example, in fact. Boxers used to go at each other bare-knuckled, and there were almost no rules. But now they wear padded gloves, compete against opponents of a similar size, and operate under many constraints* on their fighting conduct. And well-trained referees police* the matches carefully.

Maud : And yet, even with all these "improvements," boxers still get killed or live out* their lives

---

uplift : make (sb) happy or hopeful endeavor : serious effort or attempt appreciate : recognize or understand (sth) aspire to : want to have or achieve (sth) fantasize : imagine doing things that you are very unlikely to do in sync : in agreement ban : forbid (sb) from doing (sth) barbaric : very cruel bear : exhibit; show constraint : (sth) that limits your freedom to do what you want; restriction police : control (sth) by making sure that rules and regulations are being followed live out : spend the rest of your life in a specified way as semi-invalids* or mentally befuddled*.

Harold : Non-boxers die on the job as well. If someone has a heart attack at work, we don't pay much attention.

Maud : Because the job itself is not the risk factor, unless it's something like mining or firefighting.

Harold : By your logic, then, we should ban mining and firefighting as hazardous* occupations!

Maud : No. The difference is that we need miners and firefighters. We should pay them more and improve their work conditions as much as possible, but we can't get by* without them. But boxers and other athletes are just parasites*. They get paid a lot but don't contribute anything useful to society.

Harold : People are not forced to spend any money on sports; they do so because they love the competition and the excitement sports provide. And the athletes voluntarily spend years preparing themselves for their professions, long before they know if they will ever make any money at all. Amateur athletes face the same hazards as professionals, but without any of the financial rewards, but they are willing to do so because they love the game.

Maud : The risk to the innocent amateurs is just another good reason to ban the sport. Do you want your own son to become permanently injured (or worse) because he's playing some sport?

Harold : I don't want my son to be injured by walking across the street! But there's always some risk involved in doing anything. I want the officials to reduce the physical risk, especially to young players, but I don't want to deprive anyone of the challenge and enjoyment of doing what they like.

Maud : I would love to enjoy the narcotic high* of heroin, but the government bans that activity, even though some people could make a lot of money producing and distributing it. What's the difference between banning dangerous drugs and banning dangerous sports?

QUESTIONS

1. Should governments ever ban any human activity, or should people be free to make their own choices in life?
2. What sports are the most dangerous? Do they have to be potentially* fatal* in order to be regarded as dangerous?
3. As an observer or a participant, which kinds of activity do you most enjoy?

---

invalid : (sb) who needs to be cared for because of injury or illness befuddled : unable to think clearly
hazardous : dangerous and likely to harm people's health get by : be able to live or do what is needed
parasite : (sb) who habitually relies on or exploits others and gives nothing in return
high : feeling of pleasure or excitement produced by some drugs mandate : officially demand or require (sth)
potential : having the capacity to become or develop into (sth) in the future fatal : resulting in (sb's) death

Read & Discuss

Can We Call Hunting a Sport?

Carefully set a situational trap to lure* the unsuspecting prey and conceal* the danger. Give the group of hunters high-powered rifles and other technology. Allow the animal nothing but its own limited physicality, keep it as far away from the hunters as possible so it cannot endanger them, and make sure there is no way to escape. Then fire away*! The animal has no chance to defend itself or to flee from danger. Is that sport? Or is it just wanton* slaughter*, merely so the hunters can attain their trophy?

QUESTIONS

1. We designate* a lot of activities as a sport. What criteria* should be applied? What about the following (and why)? Football. Chess. Marathons. Taekwondo. Muscle building. Auto racing. Diving. Figure skating. Computer games. Poker. Dominoes. Horse racing. Gymnastics. Ballroom dancing. Baseball. Weightlifting. TV quiz shows. Dog shows. Golf. Tennis. Water ballet. Solitaire. Table tennis. Badminton. Professional wrestling. Fishing.
2. In what ways should hunting be considered a sport? Or should it be classified differently (and why)?
3. Since we no longer depend on hunting to provide us with food, what purpose does it serve?

---

lure : tempt (sb/sth) to do (sth) **conceal :** hide (sth) from sight
fire away : discharge a bullet from a gun; pull the trigger **wanton :** deliberate and unprovoked
slaughter : act of killing animals **put up your dukes :** hold up your fists to get ready to fight
wear (sb) down : make (sb) tired or weak **designate :** give a name or title to; characterize
criterion : principle or standard by which (sth) may be judged or decided

Let's Talk Funny

The Impact of the World Cup

Scientist: The World Cup has intrigued* social scientists for a long time, and we've delineated* several impacts the games bring about.

Reporter: Such as?

Scientist: First, they boost* economies around the world because people consume a lot more alcohol regardless of the game results. Second, they drastically reduce divorce rates, because people are too busy watching the games to go to court. And, third, they mark the best time for politicians to raise taxes, because people are too excited about the games to notice.

Reporter: Why don't you suggest that the World Cup committee hold the games every year?

Scientist: Because the good effects would whet* the appetite for even more frequency. Pretty soon we'd be having a World Cup every week.

QUESTIONS

1. What possible negative effects might the World Cup produce?
2. For people who are not interested in football, what do they think about the World Cup?
3. If we were forced to choose between ending the World Cup forever or not funding a cure for cancer, which would we pick?

---

intrigue : make (sb) want to know more about (sth)
delineate : clearly show or describe (sth)
boost : help or encourage (sth) to increase or improve
whet : make (sth) such as a person's appetite or curiosity sharper or stronger

Points to Ponder

1

Sports do not build character. They reveal* it.

2

Unfortunately, the only way to prove that you're a good sport is to lose.

3

When I was 60, my doctor advised me that a man my age shouldn't play tennis. So I assiduously* heeded his advice and could hardly wait until I reached 70 to start again.

4

If you're going to throw a club, it is important to throw it ahead of you, down the fairway, so you don't have to waste energy going back to pick it up.

---

reveal : make (sth) known to others
assiduous : showing great care, attention, and effort

The following sentences are all related thematically. They express a wide difference of opinions and attitudes. You may agree with some of them and disagree with others. Please discuss what you think the sentences mean and what you think about them.

5

When a man wants to kill a tiger, he calls it sport; when a tiger wants to kill him he calls it a menace*.

6

Swimming is a confusing sport, because sometimes you do it for fun, and other times you do it to avoid dying.

7

What's especially unfortunate about a team buying a pitcher for millions of dollars is that he carries no warranty*.

8

The ban on sports betting does exactly what Prohibition did. It makes criminals richer.

---

menace : threat or danger   warranty : guarantee given to the purchaser by a company stating that a product is reliable and free from known defects

1
The rules allow the wind and gravity to affect the play.
But they prohibit human intervention.

2
Congratulations on a well-fought match. Today you proved yourself to be the better boxer, but I'll try to beat you next time.
What "next time"? You're a loser! I never fight against losers. I only go after winners, so when I beat them, they know I'm the best!
I think I'm holding up the wrong boxer's arms. The other guy is the "real" winner in terms of sportsmanship, as far as I'm concerned.

3
C'mon, Granny, hit that ball!
Don't worry, Sonny, it's coming right back at you!
They play with a lot of enthusiasm, but they take a nap after every set.

4
I hate golf! It's the worst sport in the world!
But I think tossing the club would be a great Olympic sport.

5

Why did you try to kill me? I'm only acting in self-defense.

Like they say, if a tiger is chasing a group of men, you don't have to be the fastest runner—you just have to avoid being the slowest.

Don't eat me! I promise not to do it again.

6

– You should try the dog-paddle. It works better than the "man-paddle" you're using.
– You don't understand! I'm not swimming, I'm drowning. Save me!
– Do I look like some Saint Bernard with a keg of brandy around my neck, rescuing some skier in an avalanche?

7

Get up and pitch!
Throw the ball now! This is an easy out.
I can't. I'm completely worn out.
I'm getting tired just waiting. This bat is heavy.

8

We won, we won!
What do you mean "we"? I did all the work. You just came along for the ride!

ISSUE 14

Money

When I was young I had no money and was very happy, because people gave me many things. Therefore, my lack of money did not bother me. When I got older, my parents gave me an allowance*, so I finally had some money. But the having of money bothered me, because I never had enough of it. Desire always exceeded* allowance. My begging and complaints did little to expand parental generosity, so the only thing to do, of course, was to go to work and make more money. I must admit that my salary vastly outdistanced* my allowance, but it did not take long to learn that my paycheck and my bank account were altogether different things, the one being so much smaller than the other. Most of the money I made immediately went into other pockets than my own — for rent, for utilities, for food, for insurance, for car payments, and so forth, including helping my parents out with their growing age-related expenses. That state of affairs continued for a long time; even though I kept making larger sums, I never had much to show for it, as my living expenses grew faster than my raises*. Before long, I was giving free food, clothes, toys, and snacks to my own children; not long after that, I started on the allowance treadmill* with them. Oh, how I loved them and wanted to make them happy! And oh, how I hated to hear my kids complain about how stingy* their allowances were! And somehow I still had to feed and clothe them and send them to school, while also providing for my own parents. And then, the grandchildren joined the gravy train*....

When I was young I had no money and was very happy.

---

allowance : small amount of money that a parent regularly gives to a child **exceed :** be more than a particular number, amount, etc. **outdistance :** go far ahead of or beyond (sth) **raise :** increase in the amount of your pay **treadmill :** monotonous routine **stingy :** small in size or amount **gravy train :** position in which (sb) receives excessive and unjustified money or advantages with little or no effort

Comprehension

1. Do you think the writer is rich, poor, in the middle, or is his status irrelevant? Explain your answer.
2. What is the difference between a paycheck and a bank account?
3. From the context, what do you think a "gravy train" is?

Express Yourself

1. Define money in a simple, single word or a few words.
2. How does money make people happy or sad?
3. What qualities must a person have to make a lot of money?
4. How much do you save a month? For what purpose?
5. What advice can you give about good ways to save money?
6. Do you intend to bequeath* all your money to your children?
7. What can you say about how to teach children how to spend money?
8. Should kids be rewarded with extra money when they do what is expected of them?
9. Have you ever given money to charity? If not, why not? If so, what charities did you contribute to, and why did you do it?
10. Do you ever give money to panhandlers on the street? Why or why not?
11. How powerful do you think money is?
12. Is anything more important than money? If so, tell us what it is.
13. Do you think money can buy love? If so, how? If not, why not?
14. Who takes care of your family finances*?
15. Do you get a budgeted* allowance or allotment every month? How much is it? Is it enough?
16. Does a credit card merely give its possessor more convenience or does it just encourage extra, unnecessary spending?
17. Have you ever gotten a loan from a bank? Was it hard or easy to get? Was the repayment easy or hard?
18. Have you ever borrowed money from relatives or friends? Did you give them some interest when you paid them back?
19. Have you ever lent any money to anyone? Did you have any problems getting it back? Would you take a friend to court* if you couldn't get your money back?
20. Have you ever lost a large amount of money for any reason? What were the circumstances?

bequeath : give (personal property) by a last will and testament   finances : matters relating to money and how it is spent or saved   budgeted : carefully planned   take (sb) to court : start a lawsuit against (sb)

Opinion Samples

1. Money is the most powerful thing in the universe, except maybe God. People and corporations with enough money can immediately gratify* every desire and gain any objective. Money finances the arts and technological advancement, and funds hospitals and worthy causes*. Wealth can buy degrees and accolades*, win elections, corrupt governments and courts, overthrow nations. Despite what the moralists claim, money indeed buys respect and prestige, and at least the trappings* of love; as a wise man once said, "Money can't buy love, but it can rent it."

2. Money is just a convenience to make it easier to transfer one commodity or service from one person to another, but it has no intrinsic* value of its own. For that reason, everything is more valuable than money. The qualities that define the best aspects of humanity — love, trust, duty, courage, idealism, loyalty, independence of spirit, self-sacrifice, faith, hope, progress, optimism, forgiveness, humor, desire for justice, the appreciation of beauty in its many forms — all of these are so far beyond the scope* of money that there is no basis for comparison.

Dialog

What Are We Really Paying For?

Betty : I feel pretty good today.

Barney : Why is that?

Betty : I just had to sign a few pieces of paper and I made a lot of money! Isn't that enough to make anyone happy?

Barney : Hmmmm. I put in a full day's work doing what I usually do, and I didn't make any extra money at all. But I'm satisfied. I enjoy my work, and my job provides my family with all the necessities.

Betty : There's nothing wrong with that, and I'm glad it makes you happy. But you should know that it took a lot of hard work and long days and nights, and enormous personal sacrifice along the way, for me to get to the point where I can do what I did today. That wasn't easy.

Barney : I don't understand.

Betty : Maybe I can explain with an example. Some famous painter, Whistler I think, was commissioned* to paint somebody's portrait. When the patron* complained about the cost, Whistler told him that he was not being paid for the few hours it would take to do the painting itself but for the decades of training and practice it had taken to achieve the necessary skills to do it at all, and so the patron was getting an enormous bargain*.

Barney : That's a good story. I want to remember it. But there are very few people —Whistler, you, a small number of others, who have the innate* ability and ambition to reach a position that will ever allow them to capitalize on* their own skillsets* and labor.

---

gratify : make (sb) happy or satisfied cause : organization, belief, or aim that a group of people support or fight for accolade : award or expression of praise trappings : visible signs of (sth) intrinsic : belonging to the essential nature of (sth) scope : aim or purpose commission : formally ask (sb) to do (sth) patron : (sb) who gives money and support to an artist bargain : (sth) bought cheaply or for less than its usual price innate : existing from the time (sb) is born capitalize on : use (sth) in a way that helps you; get an advantage from (sth) skillset : particular combination of skills (sb) has developed

Betty : I know.

Barney : Most painters can barely make a living, although dealers often do very well selling their pieces (usually after the painters themselves have died!). Even great poets can seldom support themselves with their craft* and either have to beg or get a "real job." Police, soldiers, firefighters are all well trained, dedicated* professionals who often subject* themselves to grave danger, but they are not high income earners. Teachers, nurses, social workers are among the lowest paid professions in the world. Monks and nuns work for free. This doesn't seem fair.

Betty : Even more unfair, perhaps, are the people who get handsomely* paid just to play! You know, athletes, singers, models. They don't actually do anything constructive* but become quite wealthy.

Barney : Not all of them, of course. We just don't pay much attention to the ones who are not celebrities and superstars.

Betty : But even though I just criticized them for the injustice* of their riches, I have to put their situation in context*. There is a public that is eager to pay for the entertainment they provide, whether that is on the football field or the concert stage or the catwalk*; so if the performers did not get this money, someone else — the owner of the team, the record company executive, the advertiser — would.

Barney : Much like the painter and the art dealer.

Betty : Exactly.

QUESTIONS

1. Is there any equitable* way to share the world's wealth? Describe it, or explain why it is impossible.
2. If a person without formal credentials* can do a job as well or better than one with the proper certifications, should there be any difference in payment?
3. Is there any reason why age, gender, class, race, ethnicity*, nationality, or religion should affect equal pay? Take each category in turn and discuss the pros and cons*.

---

craft : skilled activity or profession **dedicated :** devoted to a task or purpose **subject :** cause (sb) to experience (sth) harmful, unpleasant, etc. **handsomely :** substantially **constructive :** serving a useful purpose **injustice :** lack of fairness or justice **put (sth) in context :** consider (sth) together with the related situation, events, etc. **catwalk :** raised structure that models walk along in a fashion show **equitable :** treating everyone equally and fairly **credential :** document or certificate proving (sb's) identity or qualification **ethnicity :** state of belonging to a social group that has a common national or cultural tradition **pros and cons :** favorable and unfavorable factors or reasons

Read & Discuss

Would You Like to Bet*?

No one enjoys paying taxes, though they may enjoy the roads, schools, medical care, protection, and so forth that their taxes pay for. But many people willingly pay a self-imposed*, voluntary tax called the lottery. Many of them actually pay more for lottery tickets than they pay in actual taxes, and very few of them gain any benefit from doing so.

Lotteries are inefficient and relatively expensive compared with broad, essentially universal, taxes (on incomes, for example). And, like sales and excise taxes*, they are regressive* (meaning that the ability to pay is not a factor, whereas a progressive tax*, again, for example, on incomes, may have rates that are higher on those who are better off financially). Most economists condemn* lotteries as ineffective methods of revenue collection, and moralists often condemn them as a form of gambling. But, more and more, governments are turning to* them to help balance their books, because they are easy for legislators to support, and the problems they cause are either too abstract to easily comprehend or too distant to worry about now. Nevertheless, gambling (including lotteries) is a recognized form of addiction. If governments would insist on performing the roles of drug dealer and enabler*, wouldn't they bear* the responsibility for treating the addicts they support and help create? The same should be true for encouraging gambling.

QUESTIONS

1. In your opinion, what's wrong with a "voluntary tax"? Isn't that more democratic than an involuntary system?
2. Do you regularly, occasionally, rarely, or never buy lottery tickets? What determines your level of participation? Have you paid more into the lottery than you've gotten out of it?
3. Supporters of lotteries point out that participants are actually buying hope, in the realization that they can never earn enough or save enough on their own to get the things they desire. What is your opinion of this claim?

---

bet : risk money on the result of a race, game, competition, or other future event **self-imposed :** imposed on yourself, not by an external force **excise tax :** tax on certain things that are made, sold, used within a country **regressive :** having less effect on the rich than on the poor **progressive tax :** tax that takes a larger percentage of money from people with higher incomes than from people with lower incomes **condemn :** express complete disapproval of, typically, in public **turn to :** start to do or use (sth) new, esp. when you are in a difficult situation or need to solve a problem

Let's Talk Funny

Investment Banking Reform

Man: Now is the time to reform investment banking, but is it even possible?

Friend: What do you mean?

Man: Investment bankers are infamous for their relentless* greed and for putting their own interests over their clients.

Friend: That's the very nature of investment banking, and every investor knows that. That's why people think they can get rich there.

Man: You mean they know the system is rigged* but they don't complain as long as they think they can get rich by themselves cheating other people?

Friend: That's about the size of it*.

Man: Then I think now is the time to reform people, not just the system.

QUESTIONS

1. Are there sound*, honest investment opportunities? Explain your answer.
2. Can honest people ever get rich? Why or why not?
3. Is it in the best interest of governments (and politicians) to closely regulate financial markets or to allow them to do whatever they like? Justify your response.

---

enabler : (sb) who makes it possible for (sb) else to continue behaving badly　bear : accept
death-defying : very dangerous　relentless : continuing without becoming weaker, less severe, etc.
rigged : manipulated dishonestly for personal gain　That's about the size of it : That's correct
chump : (sb) who is easy to trick　sound : sensible, correct, and likely to produce the right results

Points to Ponder

1

Too many people spend money they haven't earned to buy things they don't want in order to impress people they don't like.

2

When I was young, I thought that money was the most important thing in life; now that I am old, I know that it is.

3

The lack of money, not the love of it, is the root of all evil.

4

Anybody who thinks money is everything has never been sick.

The following sentences are all related thematically. They express a wide difference of opinions and attitudes. You may agree with some of them and disagree with others. Please discuss what you think the sentences mean and what you think about them.

5

Married men can't understand why every bachelor isn't a millionaire.

6

One's character is put to a severe test when one suddenly acquires or quickly loses a considerable* amount of money.

7

It's a kind of spiritual snobbery* that makes people think they can be happy without money.

8

Men make counterfeit* money; in many more cases, money makes counterfeit men.

---

considerable : large in size, amount, or quantity
snobbery : behavior or attitude of people who think they are better than other people
counterfeit : made to look like an exact copy of (sth) in order to trick people

1

Nobody loves me. So I robbed a bank and
I'm throwing away all my money! Maybe
they'll change their mind about me.

2

I want more money. Nothing else counts*.

You fellows will have to wait. You're not getting any of my money as long as I'm alive.

I want money! It's all that matters*!

I want bones. They're the only things that matter. Bones and more bones.

count : have value or importance   matter : be important

3

– I didn't know we could buy our own way into Heaven. I thought only living a good life could get you there.
– At that rate, it doesn't matter. I couldn't go even if it cost a few cents.
– That's too bad. But I guess in the long run* it pays to live a good life.
– In the sense of being kind and honest?
– No, of course not. In the sense of having a lot of money to spend on things to make life pleasant.

in the long run : in the course of long experience; in the end

4

– Doc, do you think you can fix me up*? I'm in terrible shape.
– I'm sure we can have you back on your feet* in no time.
– That's wonderful news.
– Provided that you have good insurance.
– No, I don't have any.
– Then you must have a lot of money, if you don't need insurance.
– No, I don't have insurance because I have no money.
– Well, in that case, as they say in the medical profession, "Cure thyself."

fix up : repair or renew   on your feet : in a healthy condition after an illness or injury

5

Before I got married, I could treat myself* to whatever I wanted. Now I never have enough money. What happened?

Hello, friends! I'm glad I ran into you before I take off* on my nice vacation next week. I'll send you pictures!

After dinner, we should go shopping.

I get to go, too! He always tells me that I'm a better companion than a wife. And cheaper to take care of.

treat myself : buy or get (sth) special and enjoyable for myself **take off :** depart or leave

6

– Help me!
– What's wrong? How can I help?
– I suddenly got too much money. I don't know what to do!
– Funny thing. I suddenly lost a fortune in the stock market, and I don't know what to do either.
– Please help me.
– How? Do you want to give me some of your money so I can start afresh*?
– No, I want you to move out of my sight, so I won't feel guilty about having so much.

afresh : once more; anew; again

7

– You look like a nice man. Can I help you? Here's some cash that might prove useful.
– No, thank you. Money is sinful*. I chose to be poor, as a matter of conscience.
– Well, then, can I give you a ride somewhere?
– That's a great looking car! Why don't you give it to me?
– I thought you hated material things.
– No, I said I hated money. But I love nice cars!

sinful : morally wrong

8

How did you become a zombie*?

The thought of money took over my whole being.

I spent my life thinking only about money. Nothing else mattered.

Really? I thought that it was caused by some kind of virus.

zombie : dead person whose body is made to move by magic

ISSUE 15
Great Inventions

Mankind's most basic inventions — the wheel, the creation of fire, the domestication* of plants and animals — occurred so far back in time we have trouble grasping* what life must have been like without them. Next in importance and chronology* came the creation of communications systems to record words and numbers. In more recent times emerged the inventions that define modern life — the printing press, the locomotive, the automobile, the airplane, the telephone, the radio, television, sound recording, space flight, atomic energy, the computer, the Internet, GPS, vaccinations, vitamins, and the application of electricity to daily living. However, we usually ignore the common objects we use every day. As I sit typing here at my desk, I see before me such ordinary items as lead pencils, ballpoint pens, spiral notebooks, white-out, cellophane tape, a stapler, ceramic coffee cups, and bifocal glasses. Outside, my bicycle is parked near my door, kept safely in place by a sturdy*, lightweight chain and rotary lock. I am very comfortable wearing my nylon clothes, with their zippers and plastic buttons, and I keep my room at a constant temperature with a heater, fan, and, occasionally, air conditioner. And I suddenly realize that, except for the ceramic cup, none of these objects in my quotidian* world have existed much beyond my own lifetime — some go back about 200 years, and most of them only decades or less.

– Do you like my new kitchen appliance*?
– It's wonderful! What do you call it?
– It's got a very clever name, I think.
– What?
– Fire.
– That's the perfect brand. I'm sure they'll make a fortune.
– Maybe we should invest?

When they said they wanted to have me for dinner, I just thought they were being polite....But, someday soon, if they keep inventing new things like this, they'll be sorry. They'll never know how to stop.

---

domesticate : tame (an animal) or grow (a plant) for human use grasp : understand
chronology : order in which a series of events happened
sturdy : strongly made quotidian : daily or ordinary
appliance : piece of electrical equipment such as a stove or washing machine, used in people's homes

Comprehension

1. When did humans invent the wheel?
2. How old are most of the mentioned items?
3. What important inventions have been left out of the discussion?

Express  Yourself

1. What invention is most needed at the moment*?
2. What not-yet-invented object would you like to see in the near future?
3. Have you ever tried to invent something, or to redesign some process to make it more efficient or safer? Discuss the work that was involved.
4. What qualities must a person possess to be a successful inventor?
5. What would happen if creative thought were to end?
6. What motivates* people to invent something?
7. In retrospect* some great inventions look very simple and easy. Why weren't they invented sooner?
8. Why do some promising* inventions fail to catch on* and just disappear?
9. What would happen if creative ideas were not protected by patent* and other laws?
10. What are the top five inventions of all time? What are the worst ones?
11. Can you think of any inventions that would solve our major contemporary* problems?

---

at the moment : right now; at the current time
motivate : give (sb) a reason for doing (sth)
in retrospect : when thinking about the past or (sth) that happened in the past
promising : likely to succeed
catch on : become popular
patent : government authority to (sb) conferring a right or title, esp. the sole right to make, use, or sell an invention
contemporary : belonging to the present time

More Talking Points (1)

Discuss the effects of the following inventions. What are their positive qualities? What bad side effects have they had?

1. Compass
2. Paper
3. TV
4. Telephone
5. Car
6. Birth control pill
7. Eraser
8. Numbers
9. Religion
10. Law
11. Atomic bomb
12. Lottery
13. Cosmetics
14. Plastic surgery
15. Pesticide
16. Canning technology
17. Clock
18. Matches
19. Medicine
20. Electric light
21. Liquor
22. Cigarettes
23. Money
24. Fast food
25. School
26. Banking
27. Beauty contest
28. Expressway
29. Air conditioner
30. Refrigerator
31. Microwave oven
32. Vacuum cleaner
33. Dishwasher
34. Batteries
35. Airplane
36. Printing press
37. Piano
38. Movie
39. Internet
40. Mirror

More Talking Points (2)

What would happen if the following things were to be invented?

1. Time machine
2. Mind reader
3. A pill that would let people live more than 300 years
4. A robot that can think and feel
5. A tablet that would supply energy to one's body (in place of food) without adding weight
6. Medicine that could cure all disease
7. Perpetual motion machine
8. Artificial sun
9. Weather control
10. Technology to revive dead people
11. Faster-than-light flight
12. Designer genes

Opinion Samples

1. Some two-and-a-half millennia ago a Greek named Hero invented the steam engine. It attracted a lot of attention but never found a use. Greek culture was based on slave labor, and the society saw nothing but trouble if its slaves suddenly had no work to perform. So the idea languished* until the 18th century, when it provided the impetus* for the Industrial Revolution. Similarly, movable type was invented in Korea but had very limited application until the idea was reconceived in Europe hundreds of years later and then proceeded to revolutionize* human culture. These are probably the most extreme examples of inventions that came into existence and disappeared, only to come back much later with profound* effect. The truth is, however, that tens of thousands of good ideas have been developed and led to working devices that never mattered because they were not practical or did not meet (or create) any widespread need. Just think of products that have recently appeared on the market but now cannot be found.

2. While it is true that an occasional "gentleman scientist" appears on the scene and uses his ingenuity to benefit mankind without thought of personal profit, such figures* are few and far between*. The fact is that, beyond the initial creative insight*, which may indeed come in a flash* of inspiration, most technological developments require enormous amounts of time and tinkering* to bring to fruition*. They require almost constant applications of trial and error. Few people are willing to invest such quantities of effort without the hope of getting something in return*, and they are certainly unwilling for someone else to benefit instead. So patents are designed to allow the ones who have had the ideas and done the work to gain whatever profit is available and thus encourage folks to make an effort to improve human lives.

languish : fail to make progress or be successful
impetus : force that makes (sth) happen or happen more quickly
revolutionize : change (sth) very much or completely
profound : very great
figure : person
few and far between : not common or frequent
insight : understanding of the true nature of (sth)
in a flash : very quickly
tinker : make small changes to (sth) in order to repair it or make it work better
fruition : successful result of a plan, idea, etc.
in return : in payment or exchange

Dialog

Nukes or No Nukes?

Margaret : I don't understand why the government is even considering the grant of new permits for nuclear plants. The ones that already exist should be closed down!

Theodore : You're always complaining about pollution, but you refuse to allow the development of the cleanest source of energy we have.

Margaret : It might be clean, but it's dangerous. Accidents cannot be completely avoided, so they will happen sooner or later. And when they do, a nuclear leak will kill thousands of people and give cancer to tens of thousands more.

Theodore : You don't think miners get injured digging for coal?

Margaret : Of course they do, but the number of deaths and injuries is pretty small compared to the potential* disaster at a nuclear plant.

Theodore : For decades, hundreds of nuclear plants have been constructed around the world. In all that time, there have been exactly three serious incidents — and all of them were quickly contained*, long before the dire* consequences you're afraid of could develop. The people who construct and operate those plants are well aware of the risks and are very careful to avoid them.

Margaret : I disagree with your facts. Two of them were quite serious, but they could have been much worse. People make mistakes. They can't help it: They're human. But when profits or other motives come into play*, the avoidance of error gets a lower priority.

Theodore : Maybe so, but I think the risks are very manageable*, and I'm not worried about a truly terrible nuclear accident. But I do have concerns about terrorists getting their hands on* nuclear materials and deliberately setting off* a dirty bomb in some city.

Margaret : It's a wonder that hasn't happened yet. But it will, mark my words*. We need to get rid of all existing nuclear waste and stop creating any more.

Theodore : How can we get rid of it? It lasts for thousands of years. Burying it is only a short-term solution, but canisters* leak and break.

---

potential : capable of becoming real; possible
contain : prevent (a serious problem) from increasing in extent or intensity
dire : very bad; causing great fear or worry   come into play : be involved
manageable : easy to control or deal with   get (sb's) hands on : find, get, or control (sth)   set off : explode
mark my words : listen to and remember what I am saying
canister : metal case that contains gas or chemical substances

Margaret : Send it up into space?

Theodore : Don't you realize how many tons of it there are, and how many billions of dollars that would cost? Besides, what would keep it from re-entering our atmosphere at some future date?

Margaret : They never should have started producing it in the first place.

Theodore : Cheap, clean, inexhaustible nuclear energy can benefit all mankind, especially as our energy demands expand and as we start to exhaust our fossil fuels. We just need to continue to make it even safer, that's all.

– What's your opposition to this nuclear power plant? Do you want to tear it down?

– It's unsafe. Any accident and the radiation would destroy all life for miles around — if the blast didn't wipe it out first.

– What if I told you they have discovered how to fix the problem? Would you be ready to accept nuclear energy then?

– How would they do that?

– Instead of uranium, they'd power it with rain. Then the only by-product would be safe drinking water.

– But then, wouldn't flooding become a serious issue?

QUESTIONS

1. Are the dangers of nuclear energy exaggerated by opponents or not taken seriously enough by its advocates?
2. Should more nuclear plants be built in your country?
3. Why don't we just use solar, wind, thermal*, or hydrogen energy instead, or some mixture?

---

thermal : relating to heat

Read & Discuss

Should We Permit Scientists to Clone* Humans?

In the science-fiction scenario, cloning is the method of recreating some long-dead notable personage*, perhaps Albert Einstein or Adolf Hitler. Or it is employed to replace a dead child, or to populate* the planet with some desired prototype like a handsome movie star. But these are unlikely to be the ways cloning is ever genuinely employed. The process is already more widespread than you may realize and is used to grow perfect vegetables or dependable* supplies of meat. Some public concern still exists about the quality, healthfulness, and economic viability* of cloned, genetic food, but for the most part it has become a non-issue for most people. The more pressing* questions have to do with human cloning, which seems different in kind than non-human cloning. Is it moral? Is it an intrusion* into divine purpose*? However, at least for now, cloning research is devoted to producing stem cells, not entire organisms; these stem cells seem to hold the key to removing or alleviating* a wide range of human diseases. If the promise holds out*, this type of cloning may in its turn* prove to be not only uncontroversial* but one of the greatest advancements in human history.

- We have a serious problem with one of our production lines.
- Which one? Pigs? Bananas? They all look fine to me.
- No. It's the baby humans!
- What's wrong?
- We got the blueprint mixed up. Instead of cloning a race of geniuses, we're turning out a whole generation of politicians.

QUESTIONS

1. Why would anyone want to clone another Einstein or Hitler? What would be some of the drawbacks* of doing so?
2. Would you want to have a perfect replica* of yourself? Why or why not?
3. Does the potential harm from cloning outweigh* any possible benefits? Discuss your answer.

---

clone : make an exact copy of (sth) **personage :** important or famous person **populate :** make up the population of (a place) **dependable :** able to be trusted to do or provide what is needed
viability : capability of succeeding **pressing :** very important and needing immediate attention; urgent
intrude : come or go into a place where you are not wanted or welcome **divine purpose :** God's intention
alleviate : reduce the pain or trouble of (sth) **hold out :** last **in its turn :** as a result of it
uncontroversial : not causing a lot of disagreement **drawback :** (sth) that causes problems; disadvantage
replica : exact or very close copy of (sth) **outweigh :** be greater than (sb/sth) in weight, value, or importance

Let's Talk Funny

The Secret to Long Life

Scientist: We have finally found the longevity* genes. Now we can realize the long-awaited dream of living 300 years or longer. Just think what that would mean!

Reporter: It's certainly a real breakthrough* in human history, but it could be a disaster for those who can't financially support themselves for such a long time.

Scientist: You don't have to worry about that. Since you live from hand to mouth*, you can't afford to implant* our newly found genes. So the problem solves itself!

– Which line do we get into?
– They don't have one for us.
– What? Why not? That's discriminatory*.
– They could have, but decided against it. According to them, at the only cost we could afford we wouldn't gain any time, not even a few seconds, and we'd actually make our lives shorter.

– 200 years. That sounds like enough.
– Longer might be better, but it would take that extra hundred years just to pay off the debt.
– I agree. But I don't understand why the cost-per-year doesn't decrease as the numbers get larger. There should be an economy size.
– Since I'm so young, I'll take the 200-year option now, figuring that by the time I get that old the costs will be way down, and I'll buy more years then.
– Am I in the wrong line? I thought this was for "Star Wars."
– I wonder if I'm doing the right thing. I'm afraid I'll look 200 years old.

QUESTIONS

1. Is long life desirable if we have to live in a sick old body or with a sick old mind?
2. Is it better to have a short life full of zest* and accomplishment, or a long one full of sadness and boredom?
3. Do we get wiser as we age or more foolish?

longevity : long life breakthrough : sudden, dramatic, and important discovery or development, esp. in science
(from) hand to mouth : without much money; in poverty implant : put (sth) in a specified place
discriminatory : not fair zest : feeling of enjoyment and enthusiasm

Points to Ponder

1

Woman's virtue* is man's greatest invention.

2

Another invention is the permanent temporary* tax.

3

We will pay a big price for an invention that will help us save time we don't know what to do with.

4

The greatest labor-saving invention of all time is tomorrow.

---

virtue : morally good behavior or character
temporary : continuing for a limited amount of time

The following sentences are all related thematically. They express a wide difference of opinions and attitudes. You may agree with some of them and disagree with others. Please discuss what you think the sentences mean and what you think about them.

5

Of all the labor-saving devices invented for women, none has ever been as successful as a devoted* man.

6

Necessity may be the mother of invention, but vanity* is certainly the father.

7

A great invention for dieters would be a refrigerator which weighs you every time you open the door.

8

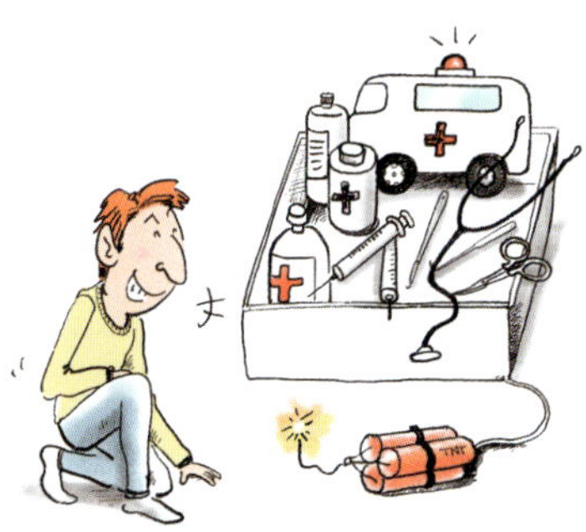

From cell phones to computers, quality is improving and costs are shrinking* as companies fight to offer the public the best product at the best price. But this philosophy is sadly missing from our health-care insurance system.

---

devoted : having strong love or loyalty for (sb/sth)
vanity : excessive pride
shrink : become smaller in amount, size, or value

1
What a great bunch of kids we have!
That's right. (I don't want to spoil his happiness by telling him that he's not their father.)

2
When you gave me so much power, you neglected to limit it. So I just keep getting bigger and stronger.
tax
fine
I might be burdened with excessive taxes and penalties, but I'll still fight you with whatever strength I have left.

3

pegged : fixed or balanced

4

rule : be a dominant or powerful factor or force

5

– Daddy, what are you doing?
– I'm cleaning the house for your mom. I promised I would.
– What's this loud thing you're using? Can't you turn it off?
– I could, but then I'd have to suck up the dust by mouth.
You wouldn't want Daddy to do that, would you?
– That would be fun! Could I watch?

6

When I finish this time machine, the first thing I'll do is go back and visit Mom to let her know how well I've done.

Hurry up, then! I want to see my first boyfriend again. He was much more romantic than you. And better looking.

7

I hate this new refrigerator! It won't open unless I can pass a weight test. And every time I pass the test and open the refrigerator, I'm unable to pass the next one.

8

Our healthcare system is so bad already. I don't believe ANYTHING can make it worse.

We concede* that our healthcare system is getting worse, not better, but it's because of people's greed. We're innocent! If you blow us up, what will save people from the many kinds of deadly diseases?

concede : admit that (sth) is true or correct

Additional Questions for Issue 01 Lifestyles

1~19 Filled

20. Among the people you know, who has the most interesting lifestyle?
21. Among celebrities in your country, who has the most appealing lifestyle?
22. Can you think of any celebrities who have a destructive lifestyle (e.g., drug addiction)? Why do you think they lead such a life?
23. If you could change anything that has happened in your life so far, what would you change?
24. What are your top three accomplishments that you are most proud of?
25. Have you achieved a good balance of work and play in your life? If not, what is lacking?
26. How important is religion or spirituality to your life?
27. How is your lifestyle similar to that of your parents?
28. How does your lifestyle differ from that of your parents?
29. At what age would you like to retire? What do you expect to do during retirement?
30. If you could exchange lifestyles with anyone in the world, who would you choose?
31. What professions have the most enjoyable lifestyles?
32. What professions have the least enjoyable lifestyles?
33. What are the advantages and disadvantages of being famous? Would you like to be famous?
34. Have you ever met a celebrity in person? What were the circumstances? Did you get an autograph?
35. Who is the most accomplished person that you know? What accomplishments have they achieved?
36. Who are the top three heroes in your life?
37. If you could have the powers of any superhero, who would you choose?
38. Who is the most powerful person in your country? Would you like to be that powerful?
39. Do you prefer to live an active lifestyle or a quiet lifestyle?
40. What is the most enjoyable aspect of your life nowadays? What is the least enjoyable aspect?
41. Do you know much about your grandparents' lifestyle? How would you describe it?
42. Is it true that the more education you have, the more you enjoy life?

What do the following quotations mean? Do you agree with the idea expressed?

43. My life is my message. –Mahatma Gandhi
44. Not how long, but how well you have lived is the main thing. –Seneca
45. I love those who can smile in trouble. –Leonardo da Vinci
46. Be happy for this moment. This moment is your life. –Omar Khayyam
47. Life is what happens when you're busy making other plans. –John Lennon
48. Believe that life is worth living, and your belief will help create the fact. –William James
49. Do not take life too seriously. You will never get out of it alive. –Elbert Hubbard
50. Your genetics load the gun. Your lifestyle pulls the trigger. –Mehmet Oz

Express Yourself

1~8 Filled

9. Do your friends have any habits that annoy you? What are they?
10. Have you ever broken a bad habit? How did you do it?
11. What are the best habits that your parents have? What are their worst?
12. Do you consider smoking a bad habit? What about drinking? Do you participate in either?
13. Do you consider swearing a bad habit? How often do you swear?
14. Do you consider gossiping a bad habit? How often do you gossip?
15. Do you consider wasting time online a bad habit? How many hours do you spend online per day?
16. Do you consider eating fast food a bad habit? How often do you eat fast food in a month?
17. Do you consider obsessive checking of your smart phone a bad habit? Do you check your smart phone more than once an hour?
18. Do you consider getting a daily hug from someone a good habit? How often do you get one?
19. Do you consider taking a nap a good habit? How often do you take a nap?
20. Do you consider the daily reading of an inspirational or religious book a good habit? How often do you do it?
21. Do you consider writing down a plan for each day to be a good habit? How often do you write down your plans?
22. Most people consider being on time for appointments a good habit. Are you always on time?
23. Many people say that saving 10% of your salary is a good habit. How much of your salary do you save?
24. Some people consider laughing a good habit because it releases endorphins, the body's natural pain reliever. How often do you laugh during a day?
25. What bad habits did high school students have in the 1950s? What bad habits do they have today?
26. In Western countries, persistent thumb-sucking by a child is considered a bad habit. Is that true in your country as well?
27. Did any of your high school friends ever try to teach you a bad habit?
28. What is a good habit that you would like to develop this year?
29. Is getting up early truly a good habit, or is it irrelevant to modern life?-at bad habits did your parents try to make you stop doing?
31. Do you have any bad habits that you hide from your romantic partner?
32. What are the worst bad habits that public speakers can have (e.g., constantly saying "uh," "you know...")?
33. What are the worst bad habits that people have about cell phones?
34. What are the worst bad habits that you see people doing in public?
35. What is the difference between a habit and a hobby?
36. Does your boss have any bad habits? What are they?

37. Does your president have any bad habits? What are they?
38. Are religious habits important to you (e.g., going to church every Sunday)?
39. Have you ever read *The 7 Habits of Highly Effective People* (1989) by Stephen Covey? What ideas does the book present?
40. What are some good habits of highly successful businesspeople that you've read about?
41. Which is more important in life, having good habits or having good luck?
42. Would you ever pay a therapist to help you break a bad habit?

What do the following quotations mean? Do you agree with the idea expressed?

43. Motivation is what gets you started. Habit is what keeps you going. –Jim Ryun
44. Ninety-nine percent of the failures come from people who have the habit of making excuses. –George Washington Carver
45. We are what we repeatedly do. Excellence, then, is not an act, but a habit. –Will Durant
46. Winning is a habit. Unfortunately, so is losing. –Vince Lombardi
47. Make a habit of two things: to help; or at least to do no harm. –Hippocrates
48. Stop the habit of wishful thinking and start the habit of thoughtful wishes. –Mary Martin
49. Depending on what they are, our habits will either make us or break us. We become what we repeatedly do. –Sean Covey
50. The best way to stop a bad habit is to never begin it. –J. C. Penney

Express Yourself

1~20. Filled

21. Who has lived the longest in your family? Do you think you will live as long?
22. Would you like to live past age 100? Why or why not?
23. Do you think that "natural foods" are essential for good health? Are you willing to pay higher prices for such foods?
24. Are you willing to eat foods that have been genetically modified (GM)?
25. What traditional foods in your country are the best for people's health? What are the worst?
26. Does your country have a problem with rising obesity? What are the causes?
27. Are you happy with your current weight? Have you ever been on a diet?
28. Do you have any friends that are overweight? Have you ever encouraged them to lose weight?
29. When you feel under stress, do you tend to eat more or to eat less?
30. What are your favorite foods that your mother prepared for you?
31. How often do you eat fast food? What are your favorite types of fast food?
32. Are you satisfied with your country's national health system? How could it be improved?
33. How much does a typical doctor's visit cost in your country?
34. If you were stranded on a deserted island, what three foods would you want the most?
35. Have you ever cooked anything for a romantic partner? What did you cook? Did he/she like it?
36. Do you think it's necessary for your wife/husband to be a good cook?
37. How would you react if your romantic partner spent an hour exercising every day?
38. Would you ever consider having plastic surgery to look better and healthier?
39. Can you explain the difference between anorexia nervosa and bulimia nervosa? Have you ever known a person who had one these diseases?
40. Do you know anyone who has had cancer? What type of cancer did they have?
41. What are the leading causes of death in your country?
42. Does your government have any programs to encourage people to maintain their health? How could the government improve its efforts?

What do the following quotations mean? Do you agree with the idea expressed?

43. A calm mind brings inner strength and self-confidence, so that's very important for good health. –Dalai Lama
44. To enjoy the glow of good health, you must exercise. –Gene Tunney
45. Happiness is nothing more than good health and a bad memory. –Albert Schweitzer
46. Early to bed and early to rise makes a man healthy, wealthy, and wise. –Benjamin Franklin
47. It is health that is real wealth and not pieces of gold and silver. –Mahatma Gandhi
48. Health is not valued till sickness comes. –Thomas Fuller
49. Treasure the love you receive above all. It will survive long after your good health has vanished. –Og Mandino
50. Natural forces within us are the true healers of disease. –Hippocrates

Additional Questions for Issue 04 Hobbies

1~15. Filled

16. Have you ever had a hobby of collecting something (e.g., coins, stamps)?
17. What are some hobbies you had as a child but no longer participate in?
18. What are some hobbies that you do as an adult?
19. What is the silliest hobby you've heard of?
20. What hobbies are helpful to other people (e.g., donating blood)?
21. What hobbies do your parents have? What about your grandparents?
22. Can you think of any celebrities who have unusual hobbies (e.g., Johnny Depp collects Barbie Dolls)?
23. Why do people start hobbies? What human need do hobbies fulfill?
24. Have you ever joined in a new hobby because of your romantic partner?
25. If you had a lot of money, would you start an expensive hobby? Which one?
26. Which hobbies are the best for making money?
27. Do you ever regret spending too much money on a hobby?
28. Does your romantic partner have any hobbies that you dislike? Have you discussed that hobby?
29. What is one hobby that is unique to people in your country?
30. What hobbies do you think are the most dangerous (e.g., mountain climbing)?
31. What hobbies can you think of that are connected to food?
32. Have you ever ended a friendship because your friend was too addicted to a certain hobby?
33. When you were young, did your parents encourage you to take up a certain hobby?
34. Do you think that sleeping could be considered a hobby, as some young people claim?
35. What sort of hobbies did people have in the past that no one does today?
36. Do you know anyone who works so much that they cannot have any hobby at all?
37. Do you have any hobbies that involve social media?
38. Which would you rather start as a hobby, going to a place of worship or going to libraries?
39. Which would you rather start as a hobby, playing baseball or playing soccer?
40. Which would you rather start as a hobby, movie watching or people watching?
41. Which would you rather start as a hobby, marathon running or collecting stamps?
42. Which would you rather start as a hobby, cooking or watching TV dramas?

What do the following quotations mean? Do you agree with the idea expressed?

43. Legendary innovators share one defining attribute. They have a lot of hobbies. –Steven Johnson
44. Find three hobbies you love: one to make- you money, one to keep you in shape, and one to be creative. –Anonymous
45. There is never enough time to enjoy what you love. –Joyce Rachelle
46. One must be serious about something, if one wants to have any amusement in life. –Oscar Wilde
47. Making money is a hobby that will complement any other hobbies you have, beautifully. –Scott Alexander
48. All the successful personalities had one common element: they all liked reading books. –Amit Kalantri
49. Hobbies are like flowers on a plant. They make the plant look beautiful and feel proud. –Sukant Ratnakar
50. I don't have time for hobbies. At the end of the day, I treat my job as a hobby. It's something I love doing. –David Beckham

Express Yourself

1~11. Filled
12. How much vacation time did your parents get when you were growing up?
13. How often does your president take a vacation? What does he/she usually do on vacation?
14. Should companies in your country be required to provide four weeks of paid vacation to workers, as is done in many EU countries?
15. Some bosses think that, if a worker takes all of his vacation time, he's not a faithful worker. Is this attitude common in your country?
16. What do you think is the ideal length for a vacation?
17. Some families use their vacation time to visit parents or grandparents. What is your opinion of this practice?
18. If you could go anywhere in the world on vacation, where would you go?
19. Are you currently saving money for a future vacation? What are your plans?
20. What are the most visited tourist sites in your country?
21. Which is better to take on a vacation, credit cards or lots of cash?
22. What are some places that you would never want to visit on vacation?
23. How much money would you need for an ideal one-week vacation?
24. Have you ever taken a cruise on your vacation? Where did you go?
25. What is one place you regret visiting on vacation? What happened?
26. Which would you prefer, to have one two-week vacation per year or several mini-vacations?
27. Do you know anyone who has won a vacation in a contest or on a game show? Where did they go?
28. Who would you prefer to take a vacation with, your family or your best friend?
29. How often do you go swimming or skiing on a vacation?
30. Do you expect to take vacations more often when you retire?
31. If you had a lot of money, would you pay for a vacation for some of your family members? Which ones?
32. What is your preferred way of traveling on a vacation: car, train, bus, or plane?
33. Do you know anyone who is overworked and never takes a vacation? What is their life like?
34. Have you ever taken a vacation in an English-speaking country? What was it like?
35. Which would you rather visit on vacation, Africa or Asia?
36. Which would you rather visit on vacation, North America or Europe?
37. Which would you rather visit on vacation, Tokyo Disney or Hong Kong Disneyland?
38. Which would you rather do on vacation, go camping or stay in a 5-star hotel?
39. Which would you rather do on vacation, go to the mountains or go to the beach?
40. Which would you rather do on vacation, go abroad or visit places inside your country?
41. Which would you rather do on vacation, go to the gym every day or sleep late every day?
42. Which would you rather do on vacation, go shopping or visit historical sites?

What do the following quotations mean? Do you agree with the idea expressed?

43. My whole life is a vacation. –Leon Bridges
44. Every person needs to take one day away. Each person deserves a day away in which no problems are confronted, no solutions searched for. –Maya Angelou
45. The best part of a holiday is perhaps not so much to be resting yourself, as to see all the other fellows busy working. –Kenneth Grahame
46. No man needs a vacation so much as the man who has just had one. Elbert Hubbard
47. When all else fails, take a vacation. –Betty Williams
48. Overworking is the Black Plague of the 21st Century. –Richie Norton
49. A vacation is having nothing to do and all day to do it in. –Robert Orben
50. When you go on vacation with people, you learn a lot about them. –Sarah Mlynowski

Express  Yourself

1~19. Filled

20 What do you think is the ideal family size?

21. How many brothers and sisters did your mother and father have? What about your grandparents?
22. How many uncles, aunts, and cousins do you have? Do you keep in touch with all of them?
23. Some countries encourage their citizens to have more children. Is that true in your country?
24. Were you, or any of your friends, ever forced to work in a family business?
25. Did your parents ever try to convince you to study a certain field, for example, medicine?
26. How common is adoption in your country? Do you think that more children should be adopted?
27. If you could change anything about your family, what would you change?
28. If you could add a brother or a sister to your family, which one would you add?
29. When you were in high school, how often did your family have dinner together?
30. What are the best habits you have learned from your family? What are the worst?
31. Would you like to have the same type of job that your father or mother had?
32. What do you usually do for your mother's birthday? What about your father's birthday?
33. When you were young, how often did you spend the night at a friend's house?
34. In your family, whose home usually hosts family events, such as special holidays?
35. Do you observe any sort of family memorial service for family members who have died?
36. Are all of your grandparents still living?
37. Who has lived the longest of anyone in your family? Do you think you will live as long?
38. In the U.S., the fourth Thursday in April is designated as "Bring Your Child to Work Day," and parents can bring a child to their job, if they want, in order for the child to experience what the working world is like. Does your country have such a day? If not, should it start one?
39. Have you ever heard about a family with a large number of children in your country? How many children did they have?
40. Is it possible to have too many children? How many is too many?
41. If you had a lot of money, would you have more children?
42. What family celebrations do you enjoy the most in your family?

What do the following quotations mean? Do you agree with the idea expressed?

43. All happy families are alike; each unhappy family is unhappy in its own way. –Leo Tolstoy
44. The homemaker has the ultimate career. All other careers exist for one purpose only—and that is to support the ultimate career. –C. S. Lewis
45. After a good dinner one can forgive anybody, even one's own relations. –Oscar Wilde
46. You don't choose your family. They are God's gift to you, as you are to them. –Desmond Tutu
47. Family is not an important thing. It's everything. –Michael J. Fox
48. No family is complete without an embarrassing uncle. –Peter Morgan
49. You can't have a happy family if you don't have a happy marriage. –Jeremy Sisto
50. Family is the most important thing in the world. –Princess Diana

Express Yourself

1~16. Filled

17. Are you still friends with anyone from high school? What about from kindergarten?
18. Have you ever used social media to reconnect with an old friend? What happened?
19. How did you meet your best friend?
20. How many close friends do you have?
21. Have you ever lost a friend who died from an illness or accident? What happened?
22. Have you ever been influenced by a friend to do something wrong? What happened?
23. Have your parents ever disliked any of your friends? Why did they dislike them?
24. Do your best friend's parents like you?
25. Have you ever ended a friendship? What happened?
26. Have you ever "unfriended" someone on social media? What happened?
27. How often have you spent the night at your best friend's house?
28. If you could be friends with any celebrity, who would you choose?
29. If you could be friends with any politician, who would you choose?
30. Have you ever lent money or borrowed money from a friend? Was the money repaid?
31. Have you ever said "I love you" to a friend?
32. How many birthday parties of friends do you usually attend in a year?
33. Have you ever planned a surprise birthday party for a friend? Has a friend ever planned one for you?
34. Do you like your parents' friends? How often do your parents get together with them?
35. Do you and your best friend have similar personalities, or are you very different?
36. What is the most memorable day that you ever spent with a friend? What happened?
37. Have you ever told a lie to a friend? Has a friend ever lied to you?
38. If your friend won the lottery but didn't give you any money, how would you feel?
39. Would you ever donate a kidney to help a friend who needed a transplant?
40. Which would you rather do with your friends, go to a baseball game or go to a concert?
41. Which would you rather do with your friends, go to a sports event or go hiking?
42. Which would you rather do with your friends, go to a movie or go bowling?

What do the following quotations mean? Do you agree with the idea expressed?

43. A friend in need is a friend indeed. –Proverb
44. Love is the only force capable of transforming an enemy into a friend. –Martin Luther King, Jr.
45. A friend is someone who knows all about you and still loves you. –Elbert Hubbard
46. A friend is a gift you give yourself. –Robert Louis Stevenson
47. If you have nothing in life but a good friend, you're rich. –Michelle Kwan
48. A true friend is one who overlooks your failures and tolerates your success. –Doug Larson
49. My best friend is the one who brings out the best in me. –Henry Ford
50. Walking with a friend in the dark is better than walking alone in the light. –Helen Keller

1~17. Filled

18. What are the most stressful jobs, in your opinion (e.g., air traffic controller)?
19. Some parents encourage their children to take a government job because you have strong job security, even though the pay is low. What do you think about this approach?
20. The U.S. has a National Boss's Day, which occurs around October 16th. Should your country have such a day?
21. How many English words can you think of for "boss" (manager, director, etc.)?
22. Would you prefer to have a high-paying job with lots of stress or a low-paying job with minimal stress?
23. What jobs are the most respected in your society?
24. What do you think is the percentage of female CEOs in your country?
25. Does a glass ceiling exist in your country? If so, in what field is it the most serious?
26. What jobs are traditionally given to women in your country? Could men also work on these jobs?
27. What jobs are traditionally given to men in your country? Could women also work on these jobs?
28. How strong are labor unions in your country? Are they too strong?
29. Would you prefer to work for a local company or a foreign company?
30. If you could move to another country, what sort of job would you look for?
31. What sort of people work on the 3-D jobs (dirty, dangerous, and difficult/demeaning) in your country? Would you be willing to do such a job?
32. What is the highest paid government job in your country?
33. Do you know what the president of your country earns? Do you think the salary is reasonable?
34. Would you be willing to work more hours on your current job in order to earn more money?
35. What sort of jobs do foreign workers do in your country? Would you ever work on any of those jobs?
36. Which would you prefer to be, a police officer or a fire fighter?
37. Which would you prefer to be, a chef or a server in a restaurant?
38. Which would you prefer to be, a taxi driver or a store cashier?
39. Which would you prefer to be, a high school teacher or an elementary school teacher?
40. Which would you prefer to be, a college professor or a politician?
41. Which would you prefer to be, an actor or a sports star?
42. Which would you prefer to be, a lawyer or a physician?

What do the following quotations mean? Do you agree with the idea expressed?

43. Great things in business are never done by one person. They're done by a team of people. –Steve Jobs
44. The difference between ordinary and extraordinary is that little extra. –Jimmy Johnson
45. Find a job you enjoy doing, and you will never have to work a day in your life. –Unknown
46. In the city, we work until quitting time. On the farm, we work until the job is finished. –John Bytheway
47. Recession is when a neighbor loses his job. Depression is when you lose yours. –Ronald Reagan
48. A dream doesn't become reality through magic; it takes sweat, determination and hard work. –Colin Powell
49. Luck is great, but most of life is hard work. –Iain Duncan Smith
50. When I was growing up, my parents told me, "Finish your dinner. People in China and India are starving." I tell my daughters, "Finish your homework. People in India and China are starving for your job." –Thomas Friedman

Express Yourself

1~25. Filled

26. Do you have any friends who smoke? Have you ever encouraged them to stop smoking?
27. Did either of your parents smoke? What about your grandparents?
28. Have you ever seen a person roll his own cigarettes the old-fashioned way, using rolling papers and loose tobacco?
29. Are you aware of any sports stars in your country who use chewing tobacco?
30. Have you ever seen anyone use snuff (powdered tobacco that is inhaled or put inside one's mouth)?
31. What sort of products are available in your country to help people stop smoking?
32. Do you know anyone who quit smoking suddenly? What happened?
33. What is your opinion of people who never drink alcohol for religious reasons? Do you admire such people, or do you think their view is too extreme?
34. What positive contributions, if any, does alcohol make in society?
35. Alcohol was prohibited in the U.S. from 1920 to 1933. Did your country ever have such a period of prohibition?
36. How would you feel about living in a country where alcohol is completely banned, such as in the Middle East?
37. In the U.S., some medicines with alcohol content, such as cough medicine, cannot be bought by minors. Is that true in your country?
38. What is the penalty in your country for a store that sells alcohol to young people?
39. What is the minimum age for buying alcohol and cigarettes in your country?
40. What is the penalty for public drunkenness in your country?
41. Can you think of any famous people who do not drink alcohol at all (e.g., Donald Trump)?
42. Does your country produce any unique alcoholic drinks that are not usually found in other countries?

What do the following quotations mean? Do you agree with the idea expressed?

43. Giving up smoking is the easiest thing in the world. I've done it a hundred times. –Unknown
44. Smoking is indispensable if one has nothing to kiss. –Sigmund Freud
45. It's better to hold a book between your fingers than to hold a cigarette. –Bista Nirooj
46. Smoking is hateful to the nose, harmful to the brain, and dangerous to the lungs. –King James I
47. I don't drink at lunchtime because I'm very weak at alcohol, like most Asians. –Ha-Joon Chang
48. Avoid using cigarettes, alcohol, and drugs as alternatives to being an interesting person. –Marilyn vos Savant
49. I do like to have fun. I don't need alcohol to have fun. –Rima Fakih
50. Alcohol is the worst enemy of the imagination. –Patrick Kavanagh

Additional Questions for Issue 10 Food

1~19. Filled

20. Would you prefer to cook at home or eat at a restaurant?
21. Have you ever worked for a company that had a company cafeteria? How was the food?
22. Who is the best cook in your family?
23. What items are you good at cooking?
24. How often do you cook for other people?
25. Can you think of any fruits and vegetables that are unique to your country?
26. Does your country require that foods containing GMOs (genetically modified organisms) have a GMO label?
27. Do you have any friends who are vegetarians or vegans? How often do you eat out with them?
28. How long do you think you could be a vegetarian (for a week, day, etc.)?
29. How often do you eat desserts? What are your favorite desserts?
30. What are some traditional desserts in your country? Are they as sweet as modern Western desserts?
31. What are some traditional types of bread in your country?
32. Are ovens used very much in traditional cooking in your country?
33. What are your favorite fruits and vegetables? How often do you eat them?
34. Where are most fruits and vegetables grown in your country?
35. If you could eat any food right now, what would you choose?
36. Which do you prefer to drink, coffee or tea?
37. Does your country have any traditional teas? How many can you name?
38. What do you usually drink with breakfast? What about with lunch?
39. Do most high schools in your country provide lunch, or do students bring their own lunch from home?
40. Do you think your mother would approve or disapprove of your food choices nowadays?
41. Did your parents ever tell you, "Clean your plate! People in Africa are starving!"?
42. Some people say that it is a sin to waste food. Do you agree with that idea?

What do the following quotations mean? Do you agree with the idea expressed?

43. All you need is love. But a little chocolate now and then doesn't hurt. –Charles M. Schulz
44. One cannot think well, love well, sleep well, if one has not dined well. –Virginia Woolf
45. There are people in the world so hungry, that God cannot appear to them except in the form of bread. –Mahatma Gandhi
46. There is no love sincerer than the love of food. –George Bernard Shaw
47. Let food be thy medicine and medicine be thy food. –Hippocrates
48. If I have one addiction in life, it's probably food. –Liam Hemsworth
49. The best way to celebrate the holidays is with some delicious food. –Rachel Hollis
50. Food is the moral right of all who are born into this world. –Norman Borlaug

Express Yourself

1~22. Filled

23. Do you have a dream car? Do you have a picture of it in your room?
24. Do you ever buy automobile magazines? How often?
25. What is the most expensive brand of car manufactured in your country? What is the cheapest?
26. Have you ever ridden in a limousine? What was the occasion?
27. How much does it cost to insure an average car in your country?
28. In Canada, if a driver gets a speeding ticket, his insurance company is notified, increasing his insurance rate. Is that true in your country as well?
29. Have you ever heard of someone bribing a police officer in order to avoid receiving a speeding ticket?
30. Can people in your country get a ticket for jaywalking (crossing the street at the wrong place)?
31. What is the fastest speed that you have ever experienced in a car?
32. What is your opinion of race car driving? Is it a waste of money and fuel, as some people claim?
33. What sort of car does the president of your country ride in?
34. Would you ever consider becoming a chauffeur (professional driver)?
35. Have you ever felt danger when riding in a car with a friend? What happened?
36. What are the penalties for drunk driving in your country? Do you think they should be changed?
37. Some people claim that red cars are more likely to get speeding tickets. Do you think that's true?
38. What is the penalty where you live for driving and using a cell phone at the same time?
39. What is the penalty in your city for riding in a car without a seatbelt?
40. Does your country require that children and babies be placed in special car seats when being driven?
41. Do you like to watch movies with car themes, such as *Mad Max: Fury Road* (2015)?
42. What do you think is the best color for a car?

What do the following quotations mean? Do you agree with the idea expressed?

43. I've always been into cars. Cars are part of our genetic makeup. It's unavoidable. –Matthew Fox
44. When you have a great car, you want people to see the car. –Andris Nelsons
45. Money may not buy happiness, but I'd rather cry in a Jaguar than on a bus. –Françoise Sagan
46. Americans will put up with anything provided it doesn't block traffic. –Dan Rather
47. With each replacement of parts, a car slowly becomes Chinese. –Mr. Kuniyasu
48. Automobiles are unreliable and dangerous slaves. They frequently revolt and kill their masters. I hate them. –Michael D. O'Brien
49. Some drivers deserve to walk. –Anthony T. Hincks
50. Take care of your car in the garage, and the car will take care of you on the road. –Amit Kalantri

Express Yourself

1~19. Filled

20. Have you ever used your smart phone to dial emergency services? What happened?
21. Have you ever owned a beeper? When was the last time you saw someone using a beeper?
22. What is the most popular manufacturer of smart phones in your country?
23. How often do you replace your smart phone?
24. Do you know anyone who absolutely refuses to buy a smart phone or cell phone? What are their reasons?
25. How long does your smart phone battery usually last?
26. Do you ever recharge your smart phone battery at work or school? Are there special places designated for this purpose?
27. Have you ever seen a person using a smart phone in public in a rude manner, such as talking too loudly? What happened?
28. Has your smart phone ever rung at an inappropriate time (in class, church, etc.)?
29. What is the penalty if high school students in your city are caught using a smart phone in class?
30. Does your local public transportation system have rules of smart phone etiquette posted? What are some of the rules?
31. Do you ever envy friends who have a more up-to-date smart phone model than you?
32. How much does a new smart phone cost in your country? What is the monthly fee for a smart phone?
33. Have you ever dropped your smart phone on the street or in water? Did it still work?
34. Are old smart phones recycled in your country, or do they just go into a landfill?
35. In the U.S., people can buy disposable cell phones (also called "burner phones"), which can't easily be traced by police. Is this type of phone available in your country?
36. Some people say that cell phone manufacturers design their products to stop working after a few years ("planned obsolescence") so that you have to buy a new phone. Do you think this claim is true?
37. Among your friends, who has the oldest smart phone model? How old is it?
38. Do you ever play games on your smart phone? What sort of games?
39. Do you ever wish that smart phones had never been invented?
40. Have you ever experienced *nomophobia* (fear of being without your smart phone)?
41. Is smart phone addiction a significant problem in your society? What sort of treatment is available?
42. Have you heard about any accidents caused by people trying to take selfies in inappropriate places?

What do the following quotations mean? Do you agree with the idea expressed?

43. We take better care of our smartphones than we do of ourselves—the phones are always recharged! –Arianna Huffington
44. The smart phone isn't a perfect device, as we all know. It runs out of battery, bandwidth, and power. It distracts us from the world around us. –John Battelle
45. Selfies are disgusting. –Brenna Ehrlich
46. My mobile phone is just an extension of my soul. –Anthony T. Hincks
47. Texting is not talking, and a phone is not a friend. –Amit Kalantri
48. A smart phone essentially creates a dossier of your travels, and consumers have no control over who will eventually see that information. –Adam Cohen
49. Pay attention to humans, not to your phone. –Abhijit Naskar
50. The smartphone is definitely smarter than us to be able to keep us addicted to it. –Munia Khan

Express Yourself

1~13. Filled

14. Do high schools in your country require students to participate in some type of sport or exercise regularly?
15. Do you think that playing sports is a necessary part of education for young people?
16. If you could enter any professional sport, which one would you choose?
17. Do universities in your country award sports scholarships to outstanding athletes?
18. Do you ever watch sports with your romantic partner? Do you like the same sports?
19. Do you ever watch sports with your parents? What kind of sports?
20. Who is the most famous athlete in your country at the moment? What sport does he/she play?
21. Some people say that golf is "a rich man's game." Do you think that's true?
22. Some businesspeople say that golf is a necessary part of conducting business. Do you think that's true?
23. Has your country ever participated in the World Cup? Did they ever make it past the first round?
24. Do you ever buy sports magazines? What sort of magazines?
25. Does your country have any unique traditional sports? Are those sports still popular?
26. What is the strangest sport you have ever watched? Would you ever try it?
27. What Summer Olympic Games does your country excel at?
28. What Winter Olympic Games does your country excel at?
29. Can you think of any athletes who later entered other professions (e.g., acting, singing)?
30. Does your daily newspaper have a sports section? How often do you read it?
31. Has your country ever hosted any international sporting events? Which ones?
32. Nowadays, some countries claim that hosting the Olympics or World Cup is too expensive and has few benefits. Do you think that's true?
33. What is the largest salary that you've ever heard of for a sports star? Do you think they were worth that much money?
34. Some sports stars earn millions of dollars but later go bankrupt. How could this happen?
35. Which would you rather play, table tennis or badminton?
36. Which would you rather play, golf or soccer?
37. Which would you rather watch, the World Cup or the Super Bowl?
38. Which would you rather watch, the Summer Olympics or the Winter Olympics?
39. Which would you rather watch, a karate match or a taekwondo match?
40. Which would you rather watch, a tennis match or a table tennis match?
41. Which would you rather watch, a soccer game or an American football game?
42. Which would you rather watch, a baseball game or a basketball game?

What do the following quotations mean? Do you agree with the idea expressed?

43. Finding good players is easy. Getting them to play as a team is another story. –Casey Stengel
44. Every strike brings me closer to the next home run. –Babe Ruth
45. Winning isn't everything—but wanting to win is. –Vince Lombardi
46. Just play. Have fun. Enjoy the game. –Michael Jordan
47. Sports do not build character. They reveal it. –Heywood Broun
48. There's three things men always talk about: women, sports, and cars. –Mario Lopez
49. To find a man's true character, play golf with him. –P. G. Wodehouse
50. I've never lost a game; I just ran out of time. –Michael Jordan

1~20. Filled

21. How much money does a person need to earn in your country to be considered middle-class?
22. How much cash do you usually carry on you each day?
23. Do you know anyone who has ever been robbed? What happened?
24. Many lottery winners end up going bankrupt. How can we explain this phenomenon?
25. Does your country have a minimum wage requirement? How much is it?
26. Do you expect your parents or grandparents to leave you some money when they pass on?
27. Where do you think is the best place to invest money: stocks, real estate, or gold?
28. Have you ever bought gold or a gold coin?
29. What is your opinion of digital currencies (also called "cryptocurrencies"), such as bitcoin, litecoin, and ethereum? Would you ever invest in any of them?
30. Do you usually pay for small purchases using cash or a credit card?
31. What is the largest purchase you have ever made?
32. How much do you usually spend on a birthday gift for your romantic partner or best friend?
33. Did your parents give you a weekly allowance when you were in high school? How much was it?
34. In most countries, it's considered very rude to ask someone how much money they earn. Is that true in your country as well?
35. Would you prefer to marry someone who has expensive tastes or simple tastes?
36. What is the most you have ever paid for a meal? Was the meal worth it?
37. What is the most you have ever paid for a taxi ride? Where did you go?
38. Do you know anyone who has declared bankruptcy? What happened?
39. In the U.S., three kinds of debts cannot be erased in bankruptcy: child support payments, taxes, and student loans. Is that legal principle also true in your country?
40. Some people say, "The rich get richer, and the poor get poorer." Do you think that statement is true?
41. Some people say, "You've got to have money in order to make money." Do you think that's true?
42. Some people say, "Money makes the world go around." Do you think that's true?

What do the following quotations mean? Do you agree with the idea expressed?

43. The love of money is a root of all kinds of evil. –1 Timothy 6:10
44. A little thought and a little kindness are often worth more than a great deal of money. –John Ruskin
45. A rich man is nothing but a poor man with money. –W. C. Fields
46. To get rich, you have to be making money while you're asleep. –David Bailey
47. Rule No.1: Never lose money. Rule No. 2: Never forget rule No.1. –Warren Buffett
48. Money can't buy life. –Bob Marley
49. I don't want to make money; I want to make a difference. –Lady Gaga
50. If you want to know what God thinks of money, just look at the people he gave it to. –Dorothy Parker

Express Yourself

1~11. Filled

12. Robert Walker invented matches in 1824 but never patented his idea, causing him to lose millions of dollars. Do you admire him for contributing to social progress, or do you think he was foolish?
13. Daisuke Inoue invented the karaoke machine in 1971 but failed to patent his idea, losing a fortune to others. How would you feel if you were Inoue?
14. Tim Berners-Lee invented the World Wide Web in 1989 but refused to patent the idea, releasing the protocol as a public service. If you were Berners-Lee, would you have done the same?
15. Jonas Salk released a vaccine in 1955 that ultimately eradicated polio, but he never applied for a patent. If you invented a cure for a dread disease, would you release it for free?
16. What electronic inventions do you use most often in your daily life?
17. What great inventions have come from your country? How many can you name?
18. What companies in your country are most likely to create new inventions in the future?
19. What is the most exciting new invention that you have heard about recently?
20. What are some great inventions that you have personally experienced at the doctor's office or hospital?
21. What are some great inventions that you have personally experienced at school?
22. What are some great inventions that you have personally experienced on your job?
23. What are some great inventions that you have personally experienced using public transportation?
24. What are some great inventions that you have personally experienced at the bank?
25. Can you think of any inventions that might help solve the problem of divorce?
26. Can you think of any inventions that might help solve the problem of poverty?
27. Can you think of any inventions that might help solve the problem of financial corruption?
28. Can you think of any inventions that might help solve the problem of learning English?
29. Can you think of any inventions that might help solve the problem of detecting deception?
30. How can your country's educational system be improved so that it fosters a more creative spirit that can lead to great inventions?
31. Can you think of an invention that frequently fails?
32. What are the most popular toys in your country? Do you know who invented them?
33. How many toy fads can you think of (e.g., Hula Hoop)?
34. Do you know anyone who made an invention? What sort of invention was it?
35. Are there any companies or websites in your country that help people develop inventions, such as Inventhelp.com in the U.S.?
36. Which would you have rather invented, the necktie or the hairbrush?
37. Which would you have rather invented, the miniskirt or the bikini?
38. Which would you have rather invented, the personal computer or the smart phone?
39. Which would you have rather invented, the light bulb or the motion picture (movie)?
40. Which would you have rather invented, the ballpoint pen or Rubik's Cube?
41. Which would you have rather invented, the automobile or the airplane?
42. Which would you have rather invented, fire or the wheel?

What do the following quotations mean? Do you agree with the idea expressed?

43. Necessity is the mother of invention. –Plato
44. I don't think necessity is the mother of invention. Invention, in my opinion, arises directly from idleness, possibly also from laziness—to save oneself trouble. –Agatha Christie
45. An invention has to make sense in the world it finishes in, not in the world it started. –Tim O'Reilly
46. To invent, you need a good imagination and a pile of junk. –Thomas A. Edison
47. No amount of skillful invention can replace the essential element of imagination. –Edward Hopper
48. Progress is made by lazy men looking for easier ways to do things. –Robert A. Heinlein
49. The world is moving so fast these days that the man who says it can't be done is generally interrupted by someone doing it. –Elbert Hubbard
50. Life is infinitely stranger than anything which the mind of man could invent. –Arthur Conan Doyle

DISCUSSION TEXTBOOKS
FROM LIS KOREA

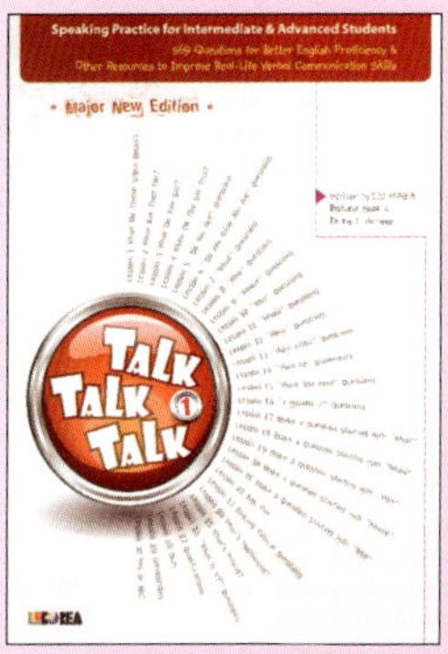

자유토론을 위한 훈련과정

Talk Talk Talk (1), (2)

- Express Yourself / Let's Talk / What Do You Think? 과정을 무리 없이 이수하기 위한 예비단계로서 자유토론에 대비하기 위한 많은 훈련과정을 포함하고 있다.
- 여러 상황에 맞는 다양한 질문을 학생들에게 던짐으로써 질문과 응답들의 패턴을 이해하고 습득하게 하고자 했다.
- Express Yourself / Let's Talk / What Do You Think?의 주요 훈련 목표 중 하나인 어떤 영어 단어나 문장을 토론자 스스로 다시 설명하는 훈련에 중점을 두었다.

Talk Talk Talk의 선생님 교재

Teacher's Guide for Talk Talk Talk 1&2

- 기존에 출간 되었던 당사의 교재 Talk Talk Talk 1, 2의 선생님 교재로 출간 되었습니다.
- Talk Talk Talk 1, 2에 나왔던 모든 질문에 대한 정확한 답변과 필요한 경우 찬반 의견들이 모두 제시되어있습니다.

DISCUSSION TEXTBOOKS

FROM LIS KOREA

중고급 토론교재의 결정판

LET'S TALK! (1), (2)

- 실생활과 아주 밀접하고 분명한 의견 대립이 나올 수 있는 주제를 선정 고급 토론 영어를 위한 기초를 가질 수 있도록 구성.
- 토론 영어의 기초 단계인 영어로 설명하는 힘을 길러주기 위해 "What Does It Mean?"을 삽입.
- Question에서는 제시된 주제에 대한 이해력 측정뿐만 아니라 한 주제에 대한 깊이 있는 토론에 대비하는 힘을 길러 주고자 했다.
- Discussion Points에서는 주어진 주제에 대한 토론 포인트는 물론이고 그와 연관된 많은 주제 제공
- Opinion Samples에서는 학습자들이 주어진 주제에 대해 토론을 준비할 수 있도록 만은 찬반 의견과 참고 의견들을 제시하고 있다.
- 어려운 표현이나 Idiomatic Expressions에 대해 각주에 충분한 영어 설명을 달아 학습자들로 하여금 이해가 쉽도록 하였다.

고급 토론 교재의 완결판

What Do You Think? (1), (2)

- Let's talk를 끝낸 학습자들이 좀 더 시사적이며 깊이 있는 문제들에 대해 토론할 수 있도록 구성
- 토론 영어의 기초단계인 영어로 설명하는 힘을 길러주기 위해 What Does It Mean?을 삽입
- Question에서는 제시된 주제에 대해 이해력 측정뿐만 아니라 한 주제에 대한 깊이 있는 토론에 대비하는 힘을 길러 주고자 했다.
- What Do You Think?에서는 주어진 주제에 대한 토론 포인트는 물론이고 그와 연관된 많은 주제 제공
- Opinion Samples에서는 학습자들이 주어진 주제에 대해 토론을 준비할 수 있도록 만은 찬반 의견과 참고 의견들을 제시하고 있다.
- 어려운 표현이나 Idiomatic Expressions에 대해 각주에 충분한 영어 설명을 달아 학습지들로 하여금 이해가 쉽도록 하였다.

DISCUSSION TEXTBOOKS

FROM LIS KOREA

청소년을 위한 토론교재

New Teen Talk (1), (2)

- 청소년 토론교재의 최고 높은 단계의 교재로서 각 권 15개의 이슈 속에 500개 이상의 토론주제를 제시합니다.
- 각 권에 포함된 9개의 포맷은 (What Does It Mean?/Comprehension/Teen Talk/Opinion Samples/Dialog/Read & Discuss/Pictures Talk/What's Your Advice?/Synopsis/) 각각의 특징에 맞는 다양하고 흥미로운 토론 주제를 제공합니다.

중급자들을 위한 토론교재

Speak Your Mind (1), (2)

- 일상적이며 쉬운 주제들을 선정하여 간결하게 정리했음
- 대표 주제에 대한 질문과 대답을 여론조사 형식으로 꾸며 독자들이 쉽게 주제에 접근할 수 있도록 했음
- 모든 주제들에 찬반 의견을 달아 독자들의 다양한 의견을 접할 수 있도록 했음

DISCUSSION TEXTBOOKS
FROM LIS KOREA

70개의 국내/국제 쟁점들로 구성된 영어토론 교재

Open To Debate (1), (2), (3)

- 70개의 한국 이슈 (1권) , 70개의 국제이슈 (2권) 그리고 70개의 비즈니스 이슈 (3권) 를 선정하였으며, 여기에 상세 주제를 더해 토론 하도록 하였습니다.
- 각 이슈에 Warm-up Dialog를 제공하여 주제에 대한 흥미를 더했습니다.
- 각 이슈에 포함된 그림과 캡션은 독자들에 흥미를 더해줄 것입니다.

설명간결한 형식의 새로운 토론교재

Express Yourself Directly (1), (2)

- Pictures Talk 섹션에서는 큰 주제에 대한 warm-up 주제들을 선정하여 그림과 함께 제시하여 본 주제에 쉽게 접근할 수 있도록 했습니다.
- Express Yourself Directly 섹션에서는 Pictures Talk 섹션에서 다루지 않은 좀 더 깊은 주제를 선정하여 심도 있는 토론이 되도록 했습니다.
- Let's Talk Funny 섹션에서는 본 주제와 관련있는 재미 있는 이야기를 실어 가벼운 토론과 함께 긴장을 풀도록 했습니다.
- What Does It Mean?에서는 본 주제와 관련된 Food For Thought를 제공하여 학습자들이 자유롭게 토론 할 수 있도록 했으면 다양한 의견이 나올 수 있는 문구들을 제시하였습니다.
- 마지막으로 Synopsis에서는 (전체 400의 그림으로 구성) 각 그림에 대한 설명을 영어로 명쾌하게 제시하여 학습자가 주제에 대한 최종 복습을 할 수 있도록 했습니다.

DISCUSSION TEXTBOOKS
FROM LIS KOREA

본격적인 비지니스 토론 교재

LET'S TALK BUSINESS
Major New Edition

15년 만에 새롭게 바뀐 Let's Talk Business -Major New Edition-의 특징은 다음과 같습니다.

- 현재 정보화 시대에 중요한 30개의 대표 이슈들을 선정했습니다.
- 각 이슈들은 Topic preview와 Warm-up Dialog에 의해 가볍게 다루어 지며, 또한 그림과 그림에 대한 가벼운 설명으로 독자들의 흥미를 이끌어 냅니다.
- 후에 각 이슈들은 전문적인 분석으로 상세하게 다루어지며, 이후 200개 이상의 질문으로 독자들의 의견을 이끌어 내게 됩니다.
- Current Hot Topic 섹션에서는 각 이슈에 대한 보충 이슈를 다루게 되며, 다시 한번 질문을 주어 독자들의 상상력을 자극합니다.

재미있는 창작 이야기로 토론의 즐거움을

LET'S TALK FUNNY

- 70개의 재미있는 창작 이야기가 수백 개의 토론 이슈와 어우러져 독자들에게 재미있게 영어로 토론할 수 있는 기회를 제공합니다.
- 또한, 우리 생활에 감추어져 있던 또 다른 50개의 Thinking Points를 제공하여 발상을 전환할 수 있는 계기가 되도록 했습니다.

EXPRESS YOURSELF 1

– 3rd Edition –

3판 3쇄 인쇄 : 2023년 5월 1일 인쇄
3판 3쇄 발행 : 2023년 5월 8일 발행
지 은 이 : 리스코리아 편집부 &
Duane Vorhees
펴 낸 곳 : (도서출판) 리스코리아
펴 낸 이 : 조은예
등 록 : 남양주 제 399-2011-000003호
전 화 : (0502) 423-7947
편 집 디 자 인 : 이명금, 전정애
일러스트레이터 : 김나나
인 쇄 : 더블비

www.liskorea.com

Once upon a time, when I was king, these ants would not have dared to play in my presence. But, now, let them be.

It's a good thing we have this chance to play. Because who knows when there will be a new young king?

I don't understand why everyone is complaining. I think the work is easy.
We do all the work! We never get any credit. I say we go on strike!
This work is too hard! I should have gone into horse racing instead of transportation.

– Do you like my new kitchen appliance?
– It's wonderful! What
do you call it?
– It's got a very clever name, I think.
– What?
– Fire
– That's the perfect brand. I'm sure they'll make a fortune.
– Maybe we should invest?

When they said they wanted to have me for dinner, I just thought they were being polite....But, someday soon, if they keep inventing new things like this, they'll be sorry. They'll never know how to stop.

Fishing is hard work, since it depends on the actions of the fish, not the fisherman. Why don't they bite?

I thought I was hungry until I heard his phone.

I guess that's why fish haven't become slaves to smart phones.

I guess human schools don't teach values.

It's a good thing (for us) that he doesn't know he can't live a simple life at the same time as a complicated, modern one.

What's wrong with him? We learned that in school.